The Early Preaching of Karl Barth

The Early Preaching of Karl Barth

Fourteen Sermons with Commentary
by William H. Willimon

Karl Barth
William H. Willimon

Translations by John E. Wilson

WJK WESTMINSTER
JOHN KNOX PRESS
LOUISVILLE · KENTUCKY

Translations from *Karl Barth Gesamtausgabe* (Zurich: Theologischer Verlag)

First edition
Published by Westminster John Knox Press
Louisville, Kentucky

09 10 11 12 13 14 15 16 17 18—10 9 8 7 6 5 4 3 2 1

Book design by Drew Stevens
Cover design by Lisa Buckley

Library of Congress Cataloging-in-Publication Data

Barth, Karl, 1886–1968.
   [Sermons. English. Selections]
   The early preaching of Karl Barth : fourteen sermons with commentary
by William H. Willimon ; trans., John E. Wilson.
      p. cm.
   Includes indexes.
   ISBN 978-0-664-23367-9 (alk. paper)
   1. Reformed Church—Sermons.   2. Sermons, German—Translations into
English.   I. Willimon, William H.   II. Wilson, John Elbert, 1942–   III. Title.
   BX9426.B3S4713 2009
   252'.042—dc22

                                                                              2009003003

PRINTED IN THE UNITED STATES OF AMERICA

∞ The paper used in this publication meets the minimum requirements
of the American National Standard for Information Sciences—Permanence
of Paper for Printed Library Materials, ANSI Z39.48-1992.

Westminster John Knox Press advocates the responsible use of our natural resources.
The text paper of this book is made from at least 30% postconsumer waste.

Contents

To Tom Long
"friends love the same things in the same way"
—Aristotle

Note on the Translation

The sermons were selected by Professor Willimon from the *Karl Barth Gesamtausgabe* (Zurich: Theologischer Verlag, 1971ff.), section 1: *Predigten*, edited by Hermann Schmidt: vol. 32, *Predigten 1917;* vol. 37, *Predigten 1918;* vol. 39, *Predigten 1919;* and vol. 42, *Predigten 1920.* Footnotes to the sermons in the German edition have been omitted. The sermon text that stands at the beginning of each sermon and quotations of biblical texts within the sermons are taken from the New Revised Standard Version. In the rare cases where Barth's German translation of the Greek significantly differs from the English in NRSV, an explanatory footnote has been added. Italicized words denote Barth's underlining in the handwritten manuscripts.

John E. Wilson

Introduction

In this assemblage of sermons we have the opportunity to look over the shoulder of a young preacher at work. We also witness a peculiar God—particularly the Word of that God—and God's people at work on a brilliant young preacher who was to become one of the twentieth century's greatest theologians. The sermons were written and preached from 1917 to 1920, a time of crisis in several ways. Although Switzerland was not a participant in World War I, which ended in 1918, the war and its terrible brutality were very close. Economic recession caused by the war affected especially the workers in the cities and industrial towns; serious social problems resulted in a general strike in November 1918. The worst influenza epidemic in modern history, which caused the deaths of millions across the Western world, also occurred in the winter of 1918. The Russian Revolution of 1917 led to civil wars in Russia that lasted until 1923. As important as the historical situation is, here we shall primarily be looking at Barth's sermons as they stand for themselves and as witnesses to the work of a young preacher committed to his task, whether the times are good or bad. For Barth, the most real crisis is that provoked by the Word.

Karl Barth's preaching is counter to just about everything contemporary preachers have been told that we ought to be in our preaching. His sermons are therefore a slap in the face, a splash of cold water, a fierce "Nein!" in the face of current homiletics. (I'm sounding like Barth).

One can see the young Barth, fresh from a dazzling run as a seminary student, making his way out to forlorn Safenwil (population 1,625) in Switzerland's Aargau on a warm July day in 1911.[1] Barth got to Safenwil two years before electricity. He was a pastor's son but had only a few opportunities to preach before his first congregation. Though nearly everyone in town was a registered Protestant (1,487, to be exact; church attendance was far below that number) Barth's church building was only about forty years old. The new structure had been built with the help of the factory owner, Hüssy, with whom the hot young preacher would eventually clash because of the preacher's leftist politics. On each side of the pulpit were inscribed two biblical texts: John 13:35 and 14:6. Barth recalled trudging to church on Sunday from the parsonage, "with a sermon in my head, good or bad, . . . behind the dung cart."

The self-described "young country pastor" (v) delivered his inaugural sermon on John 14:24, in which he confessed to his church his evangelical compulsion: "I am not speaking to you of God because I am a pastor. I am a pastor because I *must* speak of God if I am to remain true to myself." With that sermon, confessing all the frustration and the compulsion of any truly biblical preacher, Barth began his decade in Safenwil.[2] In this collection we will examine some of the most notable of those five hundred sermons. We will not only see a talented young preacher in the most important, formative years of his ministry, but also watch the gestation of one of the twentieth century's greatest and most enduringly helpful homiletical theologians. Here is the way theologians ought to be made—hammered Sunday after Sunday on the public, demanding anvil of the pulpit.

Barth confessed that preaching was the most difficult thing he had ever done. He wrote every sermon "painstakingly and down to the last detail," sometimes as if with "terrible birth pangs," beginning one sermon five times and still not being satisfied with it. Though he always produced a manuscript, he did not dryly read his sermons but delivered them in his lively, energetic, highly modulated style.

As for the congregation's reception of these sermons, Barth admitted that he demanded, though rarely received, great intellectual effort from his listeners. His sermons were long, even for his day. He always took a biblical text, focusing almost exclusively on that text, often a text of just a verse or two in length. Barth was self-conscious that his preaching demonstrated some rather dramatic theological shifts during the years at Safenwil. Beginning from the theology of personal experience, theology as existentialist angst that had so engaged him and the best theological minds during his student years, Barth's preaching eventually convinced him that he needed to find another way, a way that was more rigorously and attentively biblical, more objectively tied to the biblical text and less linked to human subjectivity, more peculiarly theological and more particularly Christian.

On the first day of August 1914 the First World War erupted. Years later Barth recalled reading a manifesto signed by ninety-three German intellectuals in which they praised the war and urged everyone to rally behind Kaiser Wilhelm II. "I discovered the names of almost all my German teachers," Barth sadly noted. It was a great jolt to the young pastor. Suddenly all "the teaching of all my theological masters in Germany" was suspect. The failure of their theology to give them the resources to withstand the ideology of nationalism and evil of war prodded the young pastor to question all the "exegesis, ethics, dogmatics, and preaching that I had hitherto held to be essentially trustworthy." Barth's youthful, refined, liberal, existential emotivism was imperiled.

Angered by the betrayal of his academic mentors and the capitulation of the church, Barth said, "I felt obliged to let the war rage through all my sermons." Finally one of his church members begged him to preach on some other subject, and Barth desisted. It's a bit disconcerting to think of this impressive theologian making a major homiletic modification at the instigation of an aggrieved layperson!

Recovering from the shock of his disillusionment with his theological teachers, Barth began to move down a path of theological reconstruction. The task of weekly proclamation of the gospel was instrumental in rescuing Barth from the collapse of his received theology. "The need for me to preach proved a very healthy corrective and stimulus in the development of my ideas. . . . Above all, it has become increasingly clear to me that what we need is something beyond all morality and politics and ethics. These are constantly forced into compromises with 'reality' and therefore have no saving power in themselves. This is true even of so-called Christian morality and so-called socialist politics."

Barth grew up in the heyday of the belle époque, in which a self-confident Europe optimistically greeted the twentieth century. Adolf von Harnack (1851–1930), one of Barth's favorite professors and a personal adviser to the Kaiser, celebrated the wonderful union between Christianity and German high culture. Harnack's *What Is Christianity?* (1900) presented a cheerful gospel of the fatherhood of God and the brotherhood of man. The "essence of the Christianity" is a matter of progressive realization of human ideals: "the infinite value of the human soul, . . . the higher righteousness, and the commandment to love."

But by the time Barth began his pastorate, what had seemed like a prosperous, secure time of cultural self-confidence was a sham. The belle époque was eventually acknowledged as the time in which a great arms race prepared the way for World War I. Nietzsche's sarcastic charge of rot at the core of German culture was recalled, and his radical antibourgeois critique was now seen to be a true assessment of German culture's true state. After the trauma of the outbreak of war and his professors' support for the war, Barth said that he and his friends began a project: "More reflectively than ever before we began reading and expounding the writings of the Old and New Testaments. And behold, they began to speak to us—very differently than we had supposed we were obliged to hear them speak in . . . 'modern' theology."[3] We see the evidence both of cultural disillusionment and of a new reading of the Bible in these early sermons of Barth.

During this turbulent period of personal struggle and theological searching, Barth said he felt as if he "battered like a bumblebee against all the closed windows." He found claustrophobic the congregation he inherited from the previous century. Barth said his people found his sermons at this time "*particularly* difficult." Eventually Barth made this period of theological disillusionment and turmoil into a time of stunning theological discovery. Though he was depressed that preaching "gets more difficult for me all the time," Barth discovered that it was this impossibility of preaching that was the true theme of theology. Painful realization of the difficulty of speaking about God is the first great step toward true knowledge of God. To say "God is" leads to being thrown into a great crisis of misunderstanding and lack of comprehension that, by the miraculous revelation of God, can be true understanding and comprehension of God. The question of the sheer otherness and distance of God is the question that Barth says he failed to understand as a theological student. "It is *the* question, which then came down on me like a ton of bricks round about 1915."

However, we must not assume that Barth's theological distress was solely related to current political events. His friend Bonhoeffer said that the true stimulus for Barth's reawakening was the Bible: "Barth's critical move in theology was not to be explained in terms of the collapse of the war . . . but in terms of a new reading of Scripture, of the Word which God has spoken in God's self-revelation. . . . This is not war-psychosis but listening to God's word. Barth does not come from the trenches but from a Swiss village pulpit."[4] It was in 1915 that Barth discovered the biblical theology of the older and younger Blumhardts: Johann Christoph (1805–1880) and his son Christoph (1842–1919).

Following Bonhoeffer, I believe that Barth made his great theological discoveries, discoveries that eventually led to *Romans* and to his entire theological project, as gifts of the weekly demand to go to the Bible and then to come up with a sermon. The brash young scholar who burst upon the theological scene in *Romans* had a couple of hundred sermons to prepare him to lead a theological insurgency. A preacher, unlike an academic theologian, cannot forever postpone a verdict, cannot avoid a weekly, public declaration of God. A preacher must preach even if the preacher feels (as Barth felt) that it is impossible for him to preach. Compelled by his vocation to preach, even amid personal theological crisis, Barth was forced into theological construction. "What we need for preaching, instruction, and pastoral care is a 'wholly other' theological foundation."

The vocation of preaching mandated that Barth and his friends take theological matters in their own hands. He said they were "compelled to do something much more obvious. We tried to learn our theological ABC all over again, beginning by reading and interpreting the writing of the Old and New Testaments. . . . And lo and behold, they began to speak to us—but not as we thought we heard them in the school of what was then 'modern theology.' . . . I sat under an apple tree and began to apply myself to Romans with all the resources that were available to me at the time.... I began to read it as though I had never read it before. I wrote down carefully what I discovered." Thus at thirty, Karl Barth began again to think theologically as if for the first time. The result was *Romans*, a discovery that I doubt could have been made by anyone but a preacher. In October 1917, during the middle of World War I, Barth asked his church council for a four-week study leave, in which he painstakingly progressed with his writing.

Romans burst like a bombshell upon the playground of European theologians in August 1919.[5] Already in this first edition *Romans* was like nothing the German-speaking theological world had seen. Now God speaks in a loud voice, with commanding authority. As is clearly evident in the second edition of 1922, the edition we have in English translation, everything is in motion: flashes of fire, stunning insight, crash forth amid sweeping claims and outrageous, unguarded assertions. *Romans* is characterized by a kind of wild, youthful excitement. Throughout there is little argument. Rather, all is breathless testimony to a vivid sense of the reality of God and the active, intrusive revelation of God. The interpreter reads the text as if he is being assaulted by God. Already in the first edition, written during 1914–18, amid the then-bloodiest war in history, a war fought between Christian nations, *Romans* sounds as if it is written by an angry young man who is breaking with his theological parentage. In the second edition the theological malcontent is clearly indebted to the great rebels of the nineteenth century: Kierkegaard, Dostoyevsky, Overbeck, and Nietzsche.[6]

Romans is great literature, a kind of theological antitheology, a Christian *Also Sprach Zarathusthra,* an exposition of a biblical text from an unashamedly theological point of view that denies being a point of view. There can be no theological argument, no rationale for the reasonableness of Paul's theology because there is no humanly derived, humanly accessible reason for believing—it's all miracle, gift, fruit of a conversation that only God can initiate and sustain.

Romans is quite a contrast to the careful, urbane, optimistic but now faded views of God in liberal theology. For the young Barth, God is energy, motion, event, and crisis. To have faith is to be swept up in God's movement, to say "yes" to the dramatic, persistent, indomitable "yes" that God speaks to us in Jesus Christ. All of our cheap human substitutes for God wilt before the wild reality of the truth of a God who *is*. All spiritualism, moralism, pietism, pacifism, even Barth's beloved religious socialism are burned away by the blast of God's reality. The Revolution that is God revolutionizes all of our ersatz revolutions.

Barth said that, in writing *Romans*, he was like a man who staggered up the steps of a dark church tower, stumbled, and instead of grabbing the safety of the handrail, grabbed the bell rope and awakened the whole countryside. In *Romans* Scripture speaks with immediacy and authority. Scripture is not of merely antiquarian interest; Scripture is where the living God speaks and presents God's self with undeniable reality. In biblical interpretation one wrestles with a biblical text, submits to its authority, bends beneath its weight, squints into its blinding light, until the walls that divide us from the first century crumble and we hear the living voice of God here, now.

"The man who sat writing his commentary was then just a young country pastor," Barth said of himself in this period. In these sermons we witness the roots of *Romans*. With the probably befuddled Safenwilers we shall hear bits of *Romans* before the academic, theological world got it. In the process we shall be reminded that all theology worthy of the name is tested in the pulpit. Academic theology always awaits a rising tide of theology in the church for only the church, that crucible where women and men are trying to live with Jesus, is the source of all the good questions for which theology tries to provide answers. Before it matures in the classroom, faithful theology is born in the pulpit.

In these sermons Barth demonstrates that he is a wonderfully energetic, singularly focused (on the biblical text), honest preacher. He clearly cares more about Scripture than for his congregation. He can be blunt with his people, telling them in one sermon, "If I wanted to be liked, I would keep quiet," though he later admits that "I often succumbed to the danger of attempting to get alongside the congregation in the wrong way." I don't see much snuggling up with the congregation in any of these sermons, either in their form or substance, but I'll take Barth's word for it.

"I always seemed to be beating my head against a brick wall," said the frustrated young preacher. He judged his hearers as those caught between the "rationalistic ideas of progress and . . . sentimental pietism." Barth said that he and the congregation stared at one another as if "looking at each other through a pane of glass." Later, when he thought of these sermons, Barth declared, "I am tormented by the memory of how greatly . . . in the end, I *failed* as pastor at Safenwil." When he visited his former congregation in 1935 as a renowned theologian, he apologized for not having preached the gospel more clearly when he was among them. "I have often thought with some trepidation of those who were perhaps led astray or scandalized by what I said at that time, or of the dead who have passed on and did not hear, at any rate from me, what by human reckoning they ought to have heard." Though they could not have known it at the time, the simple folk at Safenwil were witnessing the first stirrings of one of the century's remarkable theological transformations.

And yet we preachers will not be too troubled by Barth's gloomy assessment of his preaching at Safenwil; preachers learn from everything, learning from homiletical failures sometimes more than from the successes. And sometimes the last person to judge true success or failure in a sermon is the one who has preached it.

Those who have known Karl Barth as only the formidable, prolific, and difficult to the point of absurdity theologian will hereby be introduced to Barth the pastor. These sermons were produced in the tug and pull of life in a small congregation. More than once Barth's church council complained that he did not visit enough. He took his youthful confirmation class much more seriously than his confirmands took him. He sat through boring synod meetings whose idiotic triviality made the young pastor "want to shout something out in the room." He rebuked one of his richest, most powerful members for allowing a confirmation party at his house to get out of hand when the kids got drunk; the man withdrew from the congregation in a huff. On May Day of 1919, Barth supported the socialist-inspired general strike and marched proudly with workers behind the red flag in Zofingen; a large group left the church in protest, and the church council refused to give him that year's pay raise. He experienced the weekly grind of preaching as "a limitless problem," "impossible from the start."

Show me a pastor worth her salt who cannot connect with and be oddly reassured by Barth in these frustrations.

A major source and encouragement for Barth's preaching was his friendship with fellow pastor Eduard Thurneysen. Their hours of conversation and their lively exchange of letters (more than a thousand) demonstrate the importance of friendship for the production of faithful sermons. "He is hardly ready to settle for well-defined positions or trends," said Barth of Thurneysen.[7]

Another pastoral friendship in this period was Hermann Kutter of Zurich, who astonished Barth with his preaching: "Breathing fire, he thunders away about trenches and grenade throwers." "From Kutter I simply learnt to speak the word 'God' seriously."

In 1921, while he was working on the second edition of *Romans*—a prodigious intellectual effort for a pastor enmeshed in the responsibilities of the parish—Barth was surprised by "an enormous stone" that "fell into the pool": he was invited to assume a professorate in Göttingen. Barth became a professor after he, at least in his own estimation, failed as a pastor—not the last in that line, I can assure you.

Looking over his shoulder on his way out of town, Barth commented sarcastically that "the people of Safenwil displayed only one desire, to have a peaceful time again." He preached a farewell sermon on October 9. His text? The despairing "All flesh is grass, and all its beauty is like the flower of the field. The grass withers, the flower fades," followed by the affirmation, "but the word of our God will stand forever" (Isa. 40:6–8 RSV).

After my day as bishop, I descended to my study and translated another of Barth's sermons. Two things happened to me in the translation: I was lifted out of the muck and mire that is the daily, from one Sunday to the next, life of the church. I was reminded that church is more important than those quotidian matters that we pastors allow to consume us. In *Romans* Barth defined the church in very Lutheran fashion as the "fellowship" of those "who proclaim the Word of God and hear it" (341). Church is what happens when ordinary people are encountered by a living God who relentlessly and always surprisingly speaks, a God who does what God wants to do through words. Because of the God we have, the ministry of preaching is always prior to other ministries, the test of our fidelity, the defining act, a life-and-death matter for the church.

The young Barth reminded me that the only good reason for being in ministry is God. The God who is rendered in Scripture, and in the sermons of Karl Barth, is more interesting than I and most of the matters in which I am engaged, even more interesting than Karl Barth himself. One of Barth's great gifts is to be so utterly consumed, so singularly attentive to this God. My image of the setting of these sermons is that of a young preacher, whooping it up in the pulpit, pouring forth a torrent of metaphor mixed with questions and declarations, in fits and starts, lurching from left to right but always with vision focused exclusively upon the God who is rendered in Scripture. Barth finds interesting even the most mundane and prosaic biblical passages, shouts out to his congregation an insight derived from his study as if he has just invented fire, and week after week never fails to be shocked that this God is with us, *this* God is with us.

What the humble farmers and factory workers of Safenwil made of this weekly show, I can only speculate. Barth indicates that they were mostly befuddled or bored. The remarkable thing is that Barth is so infatuated with the biblical text that he could care less what the Safenwilers thought. I—who am so often guilty, even if unconsciously, of overconcern about my listeners' reception of my preaching—marvel. Karl Barth really is a theologian. It's all about God.

Thanks to Professor John Wilson, who masterfully translated these sermons for publication,[8] and to Donald McKim, who read my *Conversations with Barth on Preaching*[9] and encouraged me in this task. Thanks to Brenda and Keith Brodie and a gift from the Devonwood Foundation, as well as an earlier grant from the Deutscher Akademischer Austausch Dienst that enabled me to do the required research. And thanks to those who, with me, answered the call to preach. If some of my fellow preachers are half as encouraged and emboldened by Barth's early sermons as I am, I'll preach my last sermon and die happy.

Will Willimon

Mark 10:46–52

They came to Jericho. As he and his disciples and a large crowd were leaving Jericho, Bartimaeus son of Timaeus, a blind beggar, was sitting by the roadside. When he heard that it was Jesus of Nazareth, he began to shout out and say, "Jesus, Son of David, have mercy on me!" Many sternly ordered him to be quiet, but he cried out even more loudly, "Son of David, have mercy on me!" Jesus stood still and said, "Call him here." And they called the blind man, saying to him, "Take heart; get up, he is calling you." So throwing off his cloak, he sprang up and came to Jesus. Then Jesus said to him, "What do you want me to do for you?" The blind man said to him, "My teacher, let me see again." Jesus said to him, "Go, your faith has made you well." Immediately he regained his sight and followed him on the way.

Dear friends!

"A blind beggar was sitting by the roadside." What should we think about this? Here we have, in only a few words, not only the sad fate of a man but also the entire misery of humanity itself. Here we have, in all clarity and brevity, what "life" can make of us, today; what it can make of me, tomorrow; what it can make of you. "Life" is the friend of the strong, the healthy, the rich, the intelligent. It pats us familiarly on the shoulder as long as we can travel with it happily and boldly on the good and broad road, and be a little fresh with it too. Look, how they tip their hats to you! How on all sides you are surrounded with warmth and friendliness! How important you are, how much they need you, and how you can enjoy the sunshine of knowing why you are alive! Oh yes, "life" gladly plays with us in the sunshine as long as it likes to do so. But life is a treacherous and *false friend:* you never know when, in a moment, it might strike you to the ground and roll you around in the mud, if this so happens to suit its mood. Life loves change—often sudden, yet often gradual change, in which a person slowly becomes aware that, as one might say: "I'm done, it's over, I have nothing to live for." Yes, this same life that is the cheerful companion of the strong also untiringly plagues the weak. Why should you not think that you who are strong today will become weak tomorrow?

"A blind beggar was sitting by the roadside." Look at what life has made of this person! Why is he blind? Why is the sea of light that bathes

us absent for him? Why is he punished and struck down with darkness? Is it due to some guilt of his own? Or of his parents? [cf. John 9:2]. Or of his grandparents? Has he been neglected by indifferent medical doctors? Has he been in a war? Life pays no attention to such questions. Whatever the answer, the misfortune is there—too bad for you. "Now look at this!"—and it throws this miserable man on the side of the road as if saying: "*What good are you?* Look, how they all quickly pass you by." One has to pursue his business; another, his passion; another is filled with care for one's family, another is deeply sunk in high, serious thought. All that has nothing for you. As if from afar you hear the happy, eager bustle of life passing you by. It doesn't need you, who are only a blind beggar on the side of the road; it has cast you aside. And common sense whispers in your ear, "It would be better to die than to have to live with nothing more to expect from life." What do you want to do? Weave baskets? Make paper roses? Become an organ-grinder? Whatever you choose, it's nothing good and right, nothing whole and wholesome, nothing that could really make you happy and meaningfully fill your life. If one day you disappeared, no one would miss you.

Meanwhile you can *beg*, yes, be a beggar among the healthy, the strong, the rich: beg for a little attention, for a friendly thought about a poor man, for a little love, for a few crumbs from the rich table of life, where all those others seat themselves so securely, so free of care. Above all you can beg for a little money. The shadow side of life, where you now reside, is ruled by Mammon. For here all thought circles around money, however little—and how could it be otherwise? "Get what you can" is the slogan on both sides of the divide: on the side of the strong there is trust in one's own abilities and skills; on the side of the beggar one must count on the good mood of those who are happily in possession of what the beggar does not have. But it is bitter, is it not, when, so to speak, the page is turned to the *opposite side* and life forces a change, and one has to look in *this* face of King Mammon! *The world looks remarkably different* when seen in the darkness of the blind, or through the windows of a hospital or asylum for the chronically ill, or through the bars of a jail, or through the gate that separates the yard of a mental hospital from the street outside, or from the many, many back rooms and hovels of the poor. The world looks remarkably different to an older person who is without a job and wanders, searching for one, from town to town; or to a homeless family that has no choice but to apply for government welfare. It looks remarkably different to the invalid who is completely dependent on charity, or to the widow and orphan whose husband and father has been sacrificed in a war for the "fatherland."

"*A blind beggar was sitting* by the roadside." He has no choice but to accept his fate and the fact that he has been thrown off to the side of the road. He will do his best to be humble and thankful toward the pastor, the organizations that serve the poor, and the nice people who occasionally give a good word and a little help. But can he regard this world with anything but bitterness, hate, and despair? Yes, *is* this world not for him really a great suffering, a terrible injustice, an outrage? If he could, would he not cry out aloud against it? Would he not call down the righteous judgment of God against it—if he still believed in God? Now, who is right: *he*, as he sees the world; or *we*—we secure, happy, healthy people—as we see the world? We are naturally quick to say, "Oh, the world is not so dangerous! We have a thousand reasons to see the world as a good place to be. We have done a right good job of dealing with life!" And for this reason, thought out in our own comfortable experience of life, the blind beggar and all those like him must be wrong. And yet—if we could only be at peace in what we say! If only there were not something in us that thinks he is right, something that says to us, "*He* sees the world as it is; *he*, with his blind eyes, understands the world better that we do with our seeing eyes; *he* no longer allows himself to be deceived. Life at bottom is suffering, injustice, outrage! And *he* knows it, but we not yet—and that is the difference!"

And yet at times we have noticed it—by the bedside of an ill or dying person, at the scene of an accident, or when someone unexpectedly fell in sin and shame, or when we experienced something of the horror of war. And we have sighed, "What is human being!" What is human being—not just this one or that one, not just the blind beggar of Jericho, not just the cancer patient or the one who has lost everything, and not only the body that lies cold and motionless before us in the casket. No, not only these, but the question about what human being is, what we all are! Does life make fools of us all? Has it ever, even for one person, kept the promises it made? Does life have any consideration at all for us when it chooses to turn the wheel of fate, so that what was up is now down? Does it not lie in wait for each of us, with sin and care, sickness and old age? Has it not spread over the whole earth the gray, ironclad net of war and its misery, its lies, its atrocities, its death? Is it not as if we hear it laugh at all of us, all who have fallen or are soon to fall into its traps? Why may it play cat and mouse with us? What allows it to betray and deceive us as it does? Oh, if we would only consider for a moment, we would have to say to ourselves: "He, the blind beggar of Jericho, and all those like him are clearly in the right with their bitterness, their hate, and their despair." And so, as it were, we place ourselves beside them and *lift with them their accusation* against the brutal inhumanity of human beings, against the curse of Mammon, against the insanity of war, against the fate that pours sickness and care and death over us, against the injustice of life. And perhaps we now sigh with this blind beggar and cry out with him that terrible protest against humanity and the world. And in this we are right, right, right in everything—but the wind carries our words away, they fade quickly, nothing more is said, deep silence is all around us, and all remains as it was. In the distance we hear the mocking laughter of life, which continues to make of us what *it* will.

But now another passes the blind beggar of Jericho. *He too is a human being,* not an angel, not a demigod. He too is life's victim (how could it be otherwise?). He too is about to be pushed by the world to the side of the road—and to be thrown among the dead. He is not one of the strong, triumphing, and happy ones who always swim along on top of the world. He belongs neither to "good society" nor to those who climb up the social ladder with agility and guile. He has chosen a course that has no prospect of success. He has long since ruined his relationship to all the "right people." He has already suffered and will have to suffer a great deal more. He has already had enough experiences with the great injustice of life, and infinitely more such experiences await him in the future. He comes from Galilee, his home, but he is done with Galilee and Galilee is done with him. There he failed. His mother and brothers think he is an eccentric fool [Mark 3:21]; the people of his hometown have run him out [Luke 4:28–29]. Capernaum and the countryside on the Sea of Galilee have heard his call and yet heard nothing, have seen his deeds and yet seen nothing [Matt. 11:23 par.]. A small group of disciples crowds around him; they have understood him so well that they argue among themselves about who among them is the greatest— in "life" a great deal depends on that. He is followed from place to place by a curious and excited crowd of all kinds of people. They will desert him and turn against him as soon as they recognize that he does not have luck on his side. That is what happens in "life."

And now he is on the way to Jerusalem. He has no illusions about what lies ahead: Jerusalem kills the prophets and stones those who are sent to it [cf. Matt. 23:37 par.]. There await the high priests and the scribes—the whole host of church boards, sessions, and pastors who gather in the temple and are keenly interested in not letting something like this spread. There awaits Pilate, the Roman authority, with his basic dictum, "Peace and quiet is the first duty of the citizen." There await not only church and state but also the whole thrice-holy system of society, supported and borne by the people, who do not know what they do [cf. Luke 23:34]. There await the will and the power, if it must be, to erect a cross. It is also a part of "life," the way this man goes from Galilee to Jerusalem, and who now comes to the place where the blind beggar of Jericho sits beside the road. One could discuss for a long time to which of these two life has dealt the worse fate.

But this man *is in a different relationship* to life than the blind beggar. In fact a whole world lies between them. Life has made of one of them something sad and miserable, a kind of nothing; the other has taken life into his hands and is making something of it. One is the sighing creature, subjected to futility [Rom. 8:20]; the other is the Lamb of God, who bears the sin of the world [John 1:29]. How do we understand and describe this Other who was in the suffering Jesus? Oh, Jesus had already truly *seen that misery* of humanity in all its sad forms, the misery that was soon to come down on his head too. But in his eyes it was not, as it is in our eyes, the astonishing and sad thing we have in mind when we say, "Ah, the world is like that!" He sees it as something to be infinitely understood, penetrated through and through, and gotten to the bottom of. Life did not surprise him, as it ever again surprises us. Rather, he always understood it as it is. He spoke little about how it makes us fools, and never spoke a single word about things that cause so much concern, fear, and agitation in us, such as war, for example. Only on occasion does he name things as they are, as when he speaks of the rule of worldly princes and the might of the powerful among them [Mark 10:42 par.]. Or when he speaks of the fool who stores his treasures but is not rich toward God [cf. Luke 12:20–21]. A man went down from Jerusalem to Jericho—the opposite way from that taken by Jesus—and fell among robbers [Luke 10:30]. And so it is. That is the way it is in the world. That is what life does.

Jesus knew the cause and was not surprised at the outcome. God is the cause—in the singular sense that God cannot be with human beings because human beings make their life without God. With God, they could rule over life, but now they are subjected to it. With God, truth would be in their existence, but now life swindles and disappoints them. With God, their way would be straight and they would not stray from the path, but now they are subjected to life's evil vicissitudes. God is the key to life, but human beings have lost this key: what wonder that they now stand angrily before the many dark secrets of their existence. Jesus is not surprised at the suffering of the earth, nor is he surprised about what happens to him, because he sees through both and knows what is missing.

Will he now say, "*One must resign* to reality as it is?" Will he preach to the blind beggar and the whole sighing, creaturely world [cf. Rom. 8:22] the old sermon about sacrifice and patience and contentment? No, that he did not do. He was kept from doing it by what was in his conscience: deep respect for God, who will not leave humanity to itself, not let it wither in the shadows. Ever again such things are said of him: that he had compassion for the people, for they were like sheep without a shepherd [Mark 6:34]; that he stood without fear before the scribes and Pharisees and threw in their faces: "Woe to you, for you think you are serving God, yet you do so without God!" [cf. Matt. 23:13–32]; that out of indignation about life as it is he cleaned the temple with a whip [John 2:15]; that at the tomb of Lazarus he was greatly disturbed over the power of death [John 11:33, 38]; that he wanted to make his disciples active opponents of the evil spirits of this world [Mark 6:7 par.]; that he once compared himself with a strong person who attacks an armed man in his castle, overpowers him, takes away his armor, and distributes the plunder [Luke 11:21–22 par.].

No, Jesus was not the one to say, "One must resign and accept the unavoidable." Rather, he puts the power of this life against the power of God; against the power of the unjust judge he puts the power of the pleading widow [Luke 18:1–8]. He shows and gives again the key to human beings, the key human beings had lost. He promises that life must not remain as it is, that none of the dark secrets of life may threaten and depress them indefinitely, that with God life shall be different. He calls out, "God seeks you, you human beings, in your misery, God, whom you have lost. God comes to you before you do anything, and God has followed after you! God loves you in your sin and distress and will not leave you in it! Believe in God, so life will no longer be able to make of you what it will. Believe in God, and *you* will be the stronger one! Do not just accept life, and by no means accept life's meaninglessness, but accept God, who helps you!" And with this message Jesus goes to Jerusalem, yes, precisely there, not because he accepts the fact that the world is evil and will do evil to him, but in order to bring the kingdom of heaven into the world, in order to bring honor to God over against the evil powers of life that oppose God in that city. In his passion Jesus' way was not that of resignation, not that of the defeated, but of the defiant combatant who undauntedly carried forward his banner, the banner of God.

Certainly he did not do that by *crying angrily into the wind about the misery and distress of humanity,* as we often want to do. He did not do it with scolding, accusations, and protests against the foolishness and evil of human beings, against the malice of fate and the insanity of existing social and economic conditions in the world. He did not do it with a great curse on life, which is something that many noble and significant persons in their distress have finally ended their lives with. He was kept from all that by the one who lived in his heart: God, who also does not curse life. The more the misery of humanity befell him, all the more peacefully did he let it all happen. The more violently lack of understanding and evil will turned against him, the less he resisted. The higher the troubled waves of life rose around him, the more natural it seemed to him that he would be covered over by them. "The Son of Man came not to be served but to serve, and to give his life [as] a ransom for many" [Mark 10:45 par.]. He wills to drink the bitter cup, and he wills to be baptized with the hard and difficult baptism [cf. Mark 10:38 par.].

It was not easy for him to fight for God in *this* way. He had to struggle with it, bleeding both in Gethsemane and on the cross. *What* did he do? He took and bore on himself the whole terrible burden of life—godless human life, its sin, its suffering, its death—in order that what human beings do not understand in his life might be understood in his death, namely, that God is master over all these sad powers of the world, powers that we are able only stupidly to accept or bitterly to curse; that God bears this burden of our life and us all with it, while we always fall down under the burden, or helplessly try to get rid of it; that God finally is the victor over the old life and the creator of a new life, while we only know to take the old life as it is and to curse it. That was what was new: the powerful inbreaking of the kingdom of God in what he did in Jerusalem, which was more powerful there than in his most beautiful words or most astonishing miracles. He let humanity's life of sin, its life of sadness and death, crash in on him from all sides, in order to show—apparently in deepest weakness, but in truth in highest power—that God is stronger than anything and everything! Jesus suffered not stupidly and not in anger, but as the soldier of God standing at the most difficult and most exposed post and doing his duty against the evil enemy!

We understand, do we not? that this was *something different* from the suffering of the blind man who sat on the roadside and begged. The blind man and all those like him, and we too, suffer and do not know why. We do not even notice the kind of war we are in, or that in this war we must go forward and do our duty, that we must bear it in order to overcome it; that we must overcome it in order to shine forth; and that we shine forth in order to help God in the world. Jesus understood life and knew where it failed, and that God wills not to leave it in its failure, but to make all things new [cf. Rev. 21:5]. Yet not without us, but with us. He himself bravely went with this new reality into the midst of the old world; he went with his life into death, in order to work the death of death. That is what was different.

But now *something has happened* between these two sufferers, the blind man and Jesus. It was not for nothing that the suffering Christ went past the blind man, for the blind man noticed something about the one that encountered him on that road. Look, he arises from his apathetic resignation to fate! Look, he forgets his bitter accusation against God and humanity! Look, he begins to understand, from afar and yet very clearly: God can help! God will help! God must be victorious! "Jesus, you Son of David, be merciful to me!" Here it is already evident that Jesus has not traveled his difficult, lonely way in vain; here the bridge is already built from the suffering world to the salvation that God has prepared; here the blind man has already heard what Jesus through his death in Jerusalem willed to proclaim to all the world: God is stronger than anything and everything! What Jesus sought and willed to bring about through his death shines forth here already: faith, faith in God! And therefore God's help can also shine forth; here the way is now opened that rises above suffering humanity. "Then Jesus said to him, 'What do you want me to do for you?' The blind man said to him, 'My teacher, let me see again.' Jesus said to him, 'Go; your faith has made you well!' Immediately he regained his sight and followed him on the way."

Amen.

COMMENTS

Martin Luther says somewhere that a person should not be ordained as a pastor until that person demonstrates the ability to preach a full sermon on just one sentence of Scripture. In this sermon Barth does just that, expounding at length on "A blind beggar was sitting by the roadside."

Barth is known by many as a practitioner of expository preaching. He set out to take the Bible with complete and utter seriousness, leading some critics to call him a "Biblicist." Barth replied, "When I am named 'Biblicist,' all that can rightly be proved against me is that I am prejudiced in supposing the Bible to be a good book, and that I hold it to be profitable for men to take its conceptions at least as seriously as they take their own" (12).

Yet in reading this sermon it is difficult to think of it as a strict exposition of Scripture. Taking the Bible more seriously than ourselves, enabling biblical concepts to guide our thought rather than imposing our concepts upon the Bible—these are huge challenges for any preacher, even for one so determined to be biblical as Karl Barth. This sermon seems to be less expository than to be a proto-existential reflection upon a metaphor in Scripture: the blind beggar by the roadside becomes a symbol for the human condition. In his 1932 preface to the English translation of *Romans,* Barth admitted that, to be honest, when it comes to exegesis, "No one can, of course, bring out the meaning of a text [*auslegen*] without at the same time adding something to it [*einlegen*]" (ix). Still, the biblical text used here is little more than an occasion for the preacher to ruminate on the human condition in modernity. "Here we have, in only a few words, not only the sad fate of a man but also the entire misery of humanity itself." With that declaration, Barth sails into an exposition of the melancholy human situation.

Although Barth says that Kierkegaard (1813–55) did not seriously enter his thinking until 1919,[1] in some of his earliest sermons, like this one, there are statements that are strikingly similar to Kierkegaard's thoroughgoing pessimism about humanity's prospects, particularly humanity's ability to conceive of God. Christianity is that point of view that tells the somber, sober truth about the limits of human reason and goodness. Kierkegaard stressed the words of Jesus following Peter's great confession (Matt. 16:17), "Flesh and blood has not revealed this to you; but my Father in heaven." The movement from humanity to God is a journey that only God can make. Perhaps Barth was more influenced by Kierkegaard at this time than he later realized, insofar as his sermon recalls Kierkegaard's concept of "sickness unto death," which Kierkegaard taught was a means of contact with the religious. Human experiences of frustration and despair are doors into the mystery of God. According to Kierkegaard we can know God only in that dread "sickness unto death" wherein we despair of our own capacities and throw ourselves upon the mercy of the Eternal. Eventually Barth would break (in his debate with Emil Brunner) with the very idea of any "point of contact" that enables humanity to experience the divine. In time Barth would become famous for denying any capacity for revelation in humans; only human incapacity would be stressed.

But that move was yet to come. Barth is here clearly a preacher who very much desires a point of contact with his hearer's experiences. He also seems to have a clear picture of the "human condition" drawn mostly from au courant modern philosophy. He may not want to flatter or to please his hearers, but he does want them at least to admit that he is giving them an honest, truthful assessment of the human condition.

Barth begins by mocking our false sense of security. Even life itself "is a treacherous and *false friend*" that deceives us about our true situation. Just try having sickness or misfortune, and life in the world that once seemed so congenial will cast you aside like a blind beggar on the side of the road. We strive to make something of ourselves, yet life, grinding along, will eventually "make of us what *it* will," and we will find ourselves no better off than this beggar beside the road. (Just so, 1917 was the year of the Russian Revolution and widespread starvation in Germany as the war dragged to a miserable close. Is the gloom of this part of the sermon an incipient expression of the social pessimism that would sweep postwar Europe?)

Barth easily moves from anthropology into Christology as he depicts the one who comes down the road past the beggar as also "life's victim." This one too is "about to be pushed by the world to the side of the road—and to be thrown among the dead." This one walking down the road to Jerusalem has spoiled his relations with the "right people," has been tossed out of his homeland in Galilee and run afoul of the governing authorities. However, "this man *is in a different relationship* to life than the blind beggar."

This one "never spoke a single word about things that cause so much concern, fear, and agitation in us, such as war, for example" (a stunning remark to a people in the middle of the bloodiest of wars). This one did not say to the blind beggar that he ought stoically to resign himself to his situation. Rather, this one gives "the key to human beings."

What is that key that we have lost? "God, whom you have lost, . . . comes to you before you do anything. . . . Believe in God." Our relationship to the one who comes down the road is here depicted as mainly a matter of "belief," although the preacher doesn't say much about the specific content of that belief (which seems fair when the text is from Mark's Gospel: Mark presents Jesus as teacher, rabbi, but doesn't give much content of that teaching). What are we to believe about God, who meets us in this one coming down the Jericho road? "He took and bore on himself the whole terrible burden of life—godless human life, its sin, its suffering, its death." This God chose to be God "not without us, but with us." This peculiar savior is a "soldier of God" who assaults "the evil enemy." Jesus is the bridge from God to the suffering blind man beside the road. The encounter between these two suffering men ends with Jesus saying, "'Go; your faith has made you well!' Immediately he regained his sight and followed him on his way."

The year before he preached this sermon, Barth gave his soon-to-become-famous lecture "The Strange New World within the Bible."[2] Here Barth not only announced his privileging of the Bible as a source for theology but also vividly described the shape of that source: the Bible is the rumbling of an earthquake, the thundering of ocean waves. People have asked too little of the Bible, yet the Bible has within itself a wonderful ability to break free of our meager questions and pose new, more sweeping questions to us, even as we thought we were questioning the Bible. The Bible has few answers to our questions; instead, it negates our questions by raising before us the question that we have been avoiding: the question of God. This "strange, new world" did not simply want to speak to our world; it wanted to destroy and rebuild our world by the inbreaking of "the world of God." Barth, for instance, observed that the Bible was not all that helpful as a sourcebook for morality. It glorified war and had almost nothing to say about our bourgeoisie concerns in regard to business, marriage, and government. "It offer[ed] us not at all what we first seek in it." Rather, it offered an encounter with the "other" who resiliently stands against us and our questions, asserting only the tautology that devastates our theological probings: "God is God."

If this is a truly biblical sermon, it is biblical in the sense that the Bible becomes our interrogator, our accuser. The preacher clearly is fascinated by this "strange new world" within Scripture, totally absorbed by that world rather than the world in which he and his hearers live. Still, Barth rather elaborately speculates upon the situation of the blind man from one word: "sitting." He fancifully attributes resignation and rage to the blind man. From there he inflates his speculation into an entire assessment of the general human condition. Is Barth being biblical?

Perhaps the question seems odd or unfair because this mode of preaching is so widespread today, yet now without any apparent biblical control of the sermon. Come to the biblical text with some presuppositions about the general "human condition"—we are in need of more purposeful lives, we all are searching for meaning, everybody suffers at one time or another, and so forth. Then use the text as a springboard for discussing some solution to the "human condition," usually a solution that has little to do with the biblical text itself.

Barth doesn't quite do that, at least not in his resolution of the human situation. For one thing, Barth's observations about the "human condition" are more interesting than many of ours. For another thing, after the first half of his sermon, focusing on the blind man as a sort of symbol of our circumstances, Barth concentrates exclusively upon the one coming down the road who, though an outcast and a sufferer, is also the one who sees the blind man and builds a bridge to him, heals him, and wins him as a follower on the way. The one who comes down the road and reaches out to the blind man in his misery is more interesting than the blind man or his misery. The life and death of the one who comes down the road defines the significance of the life of the blind man. The sermon ends in a christological crescendo.

Barth had labored in Safenwil for nearly six years by the spring of 1917. During 1917 he made his first venture into publishing: a collection of sermons, *Seek God and You Shall Live*, published with his pastor friend Thurneysen. Thurneysen, who was quite a devotee of the novels of Dostoyevsky, made much of the "death wisdom" that comes when we truly confront our grim mortality and finitude. Most of the sermons in that collection are much like this one, beginning with a rather bleak and pessimistic assessment of the human situation, particularly our grim plight as those who must suffer and die, then moving to Christ or some aspect of the Christian faith that provides a kind of answer to the question raised by human existence.

In a few years, Barth would repent his proto-existentialist past, his youthful assumption of the need for preaching to find a point of contact with the alleged human condition. Yet already we see some familiar Barthian trajectories: Christ is the focus of the sermon, the preacher appeals for belief in Christ as the appropriate human response to Christ, there is no interest whatsoever in ministering to modern skepticism about the miraculous (how and if such a miracle actually happened). The sermon is almost pure proclamation rather than apologetic explanation, and though the sermon's existentialist analysis of the human condition sounds in tune with the best intellectuals of the day, it is devoid of interest in any of the current concerns of the day other than a fairly typical German existentialist analysis of the human condition.

In short, the sermon is not only noticeably Barth, even at this early date, but also opposed to many of today's homiletical practices. If only for that opposition alone, it is a salubrious and cautionary read for us contemporary preachers.

April 8, 1917

Colossians 2:15

Christ has led out the rulers and those with power and made a public example of them, triumphing over them. (alt.; cf. German)

Today we may all celebrate a triumph. As spring will presently draw us out of our living rooms and kitchens into the gardens, fields, and woods, where the warm sun will give us a feeling of wellness, so also the loving God now calls us out of all the houses of our opinions and thoughts and prejudices, our cares, sadness, and anger. So the loving God now draws us down from the high horse of our points of view and converts these self-formed ideas of ours, like one might turn an old coat inside out and hang it to let it air. So the loving God leads us beyond our narrow doorways into the street, so that we can see the heavens and each can face the other. God says to us, "Now let us celebrate, now leave everything *you* can do—and see what *I* can do. See what *I* have done and accomplished, while *you* were busy with figures and studies, arguing and getting angry, crying and sighing. See what *I* have done and accomplished, while you, living your lives in utter seriousness, put knowing expressions on your faces, spoke smart judgments, and threw up your hands to give them emphasis. Now look what has happened in the meantime and rejoice: Christ is risen!" This is Easter: what God has done, while we human beings ran our own ways with our hard, thick heads; while we with our little hostilities and foolishness soured life for ourselves and others; while we worshiped Mammon and waged war and suffered distress in this dark world, a world full of questions, enigmas, and difficulties. *This* is Easter: that in the midst of all that, on the third day Jesus Christ rose from the dead!

15

And now we are invited to share a little in this and to be glad in the great joy of God in heaven.

In the Bible it is called a "triumph." Do you know what a "triumph" is? In olden times when a general conquered an enemy that threatened a whole city, at his return a "triumph" was prepared for him. An honorary arch was built, as for example the one that can be seen today in Rome that was built for the emperor Titus, when he conquered Jerusalem. Through the streets and under the blare of trumpets the victor marched in a glorious procession. And after him were "led out"—to use the words of Paul in our text—the enemy's "rulers and those with power," disrobed of all their royal magnificence, stripped of weapons, now only humble witnesses to the victor's glory. Once so high, mighty, and dangerous, now they are the docile subjects of the one who mastered them! Perhaps beside them were also led out wild animals from the conquered lands, bears, lions, or wolves, or a proud elephant with its long tusks, all chained and controlled, unable to harm anyone. And these were followed by the general's exhilarated soldiers. So the general processed in his home city, in his "triumph" together with all his heroes, and the finest proof of his deeds were just those captive, defenseless rulers and those with power, the now-tamed wild animals, "made a public example" before the whole people for their joy and sport. Then all who could crowded the streets, and a great jubilation surged around the victor and rose to heaven, honoring the one who had prevented and overcome the danger that threatened.

That is Easter. God has done all that in Christ, by awakening him from the dead. The resurrection was the issue of the great battle to which Christ had gone "up to Jerusalem" [Mark 10:33 par.]. Hostile kings, now stripped and made a spectacle! Wild animals that now children can play with! What opposed him has been cast down, mastered, finished, no longer dangerous, and now in joy shown publicly. They are no longer enemies, but now subjects and witnesses of his victory, servants of his glory. And all the people may join in this joyful celebration. Now is not the time for frowning and brooding, grumbling and scrutinizing, vexing ourselves and others. For there is nothing more *against* us, but all, all is *for* us.

Oh, there was so very much against us, actually everything, *before* this victory of Jesus Christ. What a remarkable, strange, sad world was against us—*the* world, the world that is not God's world, but only that of human beings. It seems to have everything one could want, but in reality it lacks just what is most necessary and most beautiful: it has no meaning, no reason, no love, no foundation, no purpose and aim, no origin, no hope. For simply everything in this human world, even its best, its most beautiful and truthful, turns with such malice and so accusingly and dangerously *against* human being. The human being is pressed from all sides, harassed by strange and frightful things, and has no knowledge of whence they came. And the more seriously a person deals with life, the more intense a person is in thought and speech, the harder a person struggles, then all the greater do those ghosts become, until, exhausted and saddened, the person lays down one's weapons and submits to the ghosts and their might. With a faint smile and with wiser experience one resigns to the fact that there is nothing complete or perfect on earth.

We try to learn and do what is good (without God!)—and the dry finger of morality points to us accusingly: you must be good, but you are not! We look within ourselves (without God!)—and the thundering word frightens us: you are sinners! We want to work, earn, use our abilities, call something our own (without God!)—and there looms up before us modern capitalism, King Mammon, enveloping us in his claws and making us his sad and beleaguered servants. We want to know the truth (without God!)—and the dark ghost of "experience" or "scientific thought" rises up against us, and with a sullen, mocking face begins to tell us about unalterable economic conditions, about human nature always being the same and a little too closely related to the animal, and about "laws" of nature to which we are subjected and that must take their course. We want to know the last and deepest things, that which really rules our world, and to understand how all is connected (without God!)—and we encounter a long, hard series of bad, hard, empty words full of thorns and poison, all turned against us and all humanity: words like *fate, historical necessity, struggle for existence, accident, dependencies willed by God*—yes, all that!

We wish to live with and be good to our fellow human beings (without God!)—and between us and them emerge, like the stones of an insurmountable wall, the differences of position and class, of peoples, religions, parties, standpoints, education, character, and view of life. We want to love and honor our home and the people of our country (without God!)—but there are borders on our maps, and with those outside our borders we are noxious, mistrustful, hostile, and call one another German, French, or Swiss and in doing so separate ourselves from one another. We want to think about the end of our earthly, outer existence (without God!)—and must see the repulsive picture of death that has nothing to say to us but "Nothing! Finished! Take care, take care, frail little flower!" as painters of all times have painted that picture with such remarkable preference for the subject and such devotion to the task.

We want to believe in God, pray to God, be Christians (but without God! One can do that too!)—yet what we hold in our hands is a religion that intoxicates, a kind of chloroform, but no real comfort, no serious help. Instead, we hold a religion that adds to the "ten enigmas" of life a hundred more, and drives us from one disquieting thought to the next, from one unanswerable question to the next. We want—oh, all that we human beings will, wish, and want (without God!)—and ever again we come up against a concealed enemy, who seems to be hiding, waiting for us, and then triumphantly jumps upon us, as if saying, "So, you have fallen into my trap?!" And as we try to get away from one enemy, we fall into the jaws of another; freeing ourselves here, we are bound there; thinking to have found a solution on the one side, things get tangled up on the other side. As the prophet Amos once terribly but truthfully described it, "As if someone fled from a lion, and was met by a bear; or went into the house and rested a hand against the wall, and was bitten by a snake" [Amos 5:19].

Once again, the more earnestly and intensely we try (without God!), the more determinedly we fend off the enemy and try to punch a hole in the wall of our prison (without God!), all the more certainly do we become the booty of the enemy, and indeed so much so that we often are tempted to call those persons fortunate who do nothing, who are indifferent and superficial, who take nothing seriously because they never experience anything of real life. Yes, as if among all those invisible animals that surround us, we could do nothing, as if indifferent, superficial stupidity were not the worst deception with which we can deceive ourselves!—All those are the "rulers and those with power" that are arrayed against us in *the* world, which is only the world of human beings and not the world of God! But this world *is* actually no longer, but *was*! *When?* When Christ had not yet fought and won! *Where? Before* the resurrection of Jesus Christ from the dead! Hear the Easter message: This world is no longer! A new world has broken in, as on the first day of creation! The old has passed away! "Christ is risen, joy to the mortals, round whom the pale, creeping, ruinous privations entwined!"[1]

For "Christ has led out the rulers and those with power and made a public example of them, triumphing over them!" How has he conquered these enemies of human beings and placed them in his service?

Seemingly he has done nothing at all. He has not done it by demonstrating to human beings either good or evil; nor has he founded a school for their enlightenment and education. He has been neither a reformer nor a revolutionary. He has not been zealous for faith in opposition to unbelief and even less for the church against the unchurched. He has neither brooded over problems nor come up with new and ingenious solutions. He has not proclaimed a way to live according to nature, nor preached world peace, nor even founded a new religion. And yet he has done *more* than all that. He knew and willed only *one* thing, but everything was in this one thing. He proclaimed *one* word: God! He had and needed *one* power, the power of God. He expected *one* action for his life and for the future: the action of God! He wanted to know about only *one* key to the enigmatic locked doors of the world. He risked and believed and did only one thing.

What was new in Jesus was only this word, this power, this hope: God! With penetrating vision he saw what we do not see: that God is really new for the world, not someone long since known and used to. We have thought of everything there is to think about, but not of God. We have talked about everything there is to talk about, but never has our talk been about God. We have risked and done everything there is to risk and do, but we have not believed in God. This new living God, whom the world and we lack and of whom we hardly have the faintest inkling—Jesus had this living God. Moses and the prophets desired, honored, obeyed, and cried out to God. But Jesus had this living God. God was in him. He called God Father and himself the Son of the Father. And only with this one reality, God, he went into the conflict with the fearsome enemies of human being. But why do I say fearsome?—that is only true for us: for God nothing is fearsome. God does not fear.

And therefore Jesus *was* already the victor, when he "went up to Jerusalem" to enter this conflict, because his business was God's business. For this reason Jesus was so completely different from all the other good, noble, and excellent persons who have ever lived. He cannot be characterized with the words we use to characterize them: *serious, solemn, grim, intense, excited, partisan, aggressive*, even though all "rulers and those with power" in our human world stood against him. In the face of the enemy, where pain over the distress of the world would almost tear him apart, he maintains within himself something free and full of understanding, something gracious and superior, something almost smiling within him. Think of how he spoke, in the presence of

Judas, with his foolish disciples on that last evening, opening his heart to them! That has only *one* explanation: that he fought for God, that he had only *one* goal: God's reality, lordship, and kingdom. Whoever fights for this *has* the victory already in advance. One need not take the "rulers and those with power" so very seriously. They are serious matters only if God is not.

If God is, then good is no longer difficult and evil no longer frightening. If God is, then sin is no longer damned but forgiven. If God is, then what *is* and what *can* Mammon, this murder of souls, be? If God is, then what is the "experience" and what are the social and economic "conditions" of this world? If God is, then how small and unimportant become the human things that separate us from one another. How can death remain death, as the bands and boundaries of the religions and the confessions of the churches break apart, as our whole tiresome brain racking over the highest things happily ceases, as all of life becomes wonderfully simple? Everywhere an awakening out of feverish dreams! Everywhere confusions come to clarity! Everywhere a restful, happy overview and understanding of life! Everywhere the happy, patient certainty: "I know that my Redeemer lives!" [Job 19:25]. In the words of the hymn, "Take Heart, Believers" [Ermuntert euch, ihr Frommen]: "He will not long delay, do not fall asleep! The trees are greening, the most beautiful shine of spring promises new life, and evening sunset reflects from afar the beautiful day that makes the darkness fade away."

Yes, *if God is!* Oh, you are entirely right: all that is mist and smoke, fantasy and dream—if God is not. If God is not, then the world is and remains the "reality" we know it well enough to be, and no one needs to remind us of it. But now Jesus has fought, has fully committed himself to the *reality of God.* Jesus has carried the flag into the poor world that sighs under its "rulers and those with power": *God is!* And whoever carries *this* flag is the victor already *before* the fight.

That is why *before* Good Friday Jesus could give his disciples the Supper: my body—my blood—for many!—as the sign of victory, a victory into which he drew them. Therefore Easter was, resurrection was already on Good Friday, already in the darkest hour, as Jesus cried out on the cross, "My God, my God, why have you forsaken me?" [Mark 15:34 par.]. For that was not a "No," but the last and loudest "Yes!" Yes, God is! even when the ever-higher-climbing waves of the world and its distress break over hopeless human being. *I* am abandoned, but *you*, God, you *are*, you *are* God! And just that was the victory of Jesus. With God he was victorious. God was victorious in him.

God was stronger than human sin, for Jesus could pray on the cross for sinners [Luke 23:34]. God was stronger than fate, for even in deepest distress Jesus did not resign to his fate, but commended his spirit into the hands of the Father [Luke 23:46]. God was stronger than Mammon, for in the suffering of Jesus *that* came to light which holds and binds human beings *stronger* than the cursed "mine" and "yours" that separates us: stronger was the love that made him a brother among brothers and sisters. God was stronger than all powers of the devil that hinder our brother- and sisterhood and would tear it apart, for the heavenly power that Jesus always had and ever again demonstrated unites human beings over and beyond all forms of separation. God was stronger than death, for Jesus has in his death put death itself to death; whoever so dies, does not die, even if he should die! [cf. John 11:25]. God was stronger than religion and church, for in the cross of Christ, God's win was act and life over the sacrifices, edifications, prayers, and sermons of an unsaved humanity. God is stronger! The "rulers and those in power" are defeated; in Christ the victory of God has broken in over them! Resurrection! That is the word that Jesus has spoken once and for all.

On the third day precisely this word was heard at the grave of Jesus: God is stronger! Much has been said about and, sadly, also fought over *how* it could have happened. How should we, with our usual thoughts about life and death, spirit and body, describe this event? How, with our usual concepts of the beyond and of miracles? This event bursts our usual thoughts, so that we, in astonishment and confusion, must seek new thoughts! That we are here at a loss is only too understandable, because we have until now been at a complete loss with regard to God. In the Bible it is said so very simply: "Their eyes were opened" [Luke 24:31]. Yes, that is it—the solution of the enigma at the grave of Jesus: eyes that see how God in Christ is victorious over all that plagues, depresses, frightens, and shames us human beings, victorious also over the last enemy, death [cf. 1 Cor. 15:26]. "If God is for us, who is against us?" [Rom. 8:31]. The grave, the decay, the laws of nature? What is death, if God is?

That is the triumph in which we today may join. We are invited to be spectators, to view this triumph. An old world has collapsed, and in Christ a new world has opened. The old person (without God!) has been carried to the grave; the new person in God has entered existence in Christ. How simple, how innocuous all that frightened us has become—if we see it *from that viewpoint*! How all that frightened us is led out publicly: subjected kings, tamed beasts!

We are invited to be spectators. We have *heard* again how it really *is*.
At least it has been *said*! But can we *only* be spectators, and can we *only*
listen? Does God's joy over God's victory have anything to do with us?
Do we want simply to return again to the old world, the world without
God, to again tremble and quake before the "rulers and those with
power"? Or will something in us stir and move, so that we let this new
thing that has become truth in Christ also become new in us, so that we
hear it in our deepest souls? Yes, God is stronger! Christ is risen! And
with this God let us move, get up, and do good deeds! [cf. Pss. 60:12;
108:13]. Indeed, why should we not let ourselves be drawn into the
victory that we celebrate today?

COMMENTS

Barth said that as he worked on *Romans* during 1917, he could almost
"hear the sound of the guns booming away in the north" (v). Amid the
wreckage, disillusionment, and gloom engendered by the war, on Easter Barth stands and announces triumph. There is no hope for human
perfectibility or progress: that failed nineteenth-century project leads to
the wretchedness of Verdun and the Marne. Such vain human hopeful-
ness withers before the grand victory of God in the resurrection.

Barth begins his Easter sermon on some suspicious ground—with
talk of spring and "the warm sun" that gives "us a feeling of wellness."
Is Barth headed for commonplace and conventional drivel that tries to
compare Easter with the butterfly's emergence from the cocoon, the
return of the robin in the spring to the valleys of Switzerland? Of course
not. The preacher plays a sly trick. Just as spring leads these shivering
Swiss out of inhospitable winter into the welcoming sun, so in Easter
"God leads us beyond our narrow doorways into the street," saying,
"Leave everything *you* can do—and see what *I* can do." This sermon is
destined to be about God.

The preacher admits that we are in quite a fix in the world "*before
this victory of Jesus Christ*," in the humanly derived world that is so
hostile to our humanity. Barth is certainly speaking to a world after
Easter, but it is a world that is "sad" because it does not yet know
of God's great victory. Easter is a fact, but a fact that is not yet fully
accomplished due to our baffling lack of acknowledgment of the fact.

Then Barth catalogs evidence of our sin, a rather unconventional cat-
alog of human depravity: capitalism, scientific thought, and social and

economic conditions. What the world regards as progress and achieve-ment, the preacher scorns as sin. Of particular note for the preacher is the way the modern world hedges us in with unalterable "laws" of nature, "unalterable economic conditions," "fate," and "struggle for existence." Darwin and Marx, soon to by joined by Freud, depicted a world of fate, of biological necessity, of grim determinism and cease-less, insoluble class struggle. This is the world that doesn't know God.

Not content to attack secular godlessness and its bitter fruit, Barth ridicules our Christianity too, the faith "without God" that "intox-icates, a kind of chloroform, but no real comfort, no serious help." Then he exuberantly announces, "This world is no longer!" The Easter message is that it's a whole new world, as if it is Genesis 1 all over again and a totally new creation. How? What did Christ do to obtain such remarkable triumph? He was "neither a reformer nor a revolutionary." He founded neither a school nor even a new religion. "He proclaimed *one* word: God!"

The risen Christ is here portrayed as a preacher who preached a one-word sermon: "God!" Christ embodied and enacted total depen-dence on God, total trust, complete obedience, and he was vindicated by being raised from the dead.

As Barth preached this Easter sermon, European intellectuals were awakening to a newfound preoccupation with the subjective and the unconscious as the vast new frontier. So 1917 was not only the year that Barth preached this sermon but also the year that Freud published *Introduction to Psychoanalysis* and Jung, *The Unconscious.* While there is no reason to think that the young Barth was aware of their work at this early date, Barth could certainly have wandered into this newly discovered subjective terrain as a means of making the faith credible. Kant had left theological truth claims little territory in which to speak save the subjective.

Instead, we see Barth taking another path. Here he stresses, not the power of human subjectivity in linking us to some vague divine, but rather the overwhelming objectivity of divine victory in resurrection. In other words this sermon shows the young preacher leaving one world and headed for another.[2] I wonder if the weekly task of having to be encountered by a text of Scripture, having to stand up and preach the text, was a major factor in the young Barth's restiveness with the theol-ogy he had imbibed in seminary.

Though Barth didn't say it here, we have learned that a major cause of war is that war has become our main attempt to secure ourselves, to win some sort of triumph on our own terms. People who have no faith in the ultimate triumph of God must therefore secure some sort of triumph on their own, and in our world, in the modern nation-state, we have no means of triumph except war. As Stanley Hauerwas has said, the most tragic day in our nation's history was not September 11, 2001, but rather September 12, when we responded to a grave act of criminal injustice, not with hope for or expectation in the triumph of God, but rather with unprecedented military force. It's the only means of transcendence available to a people who no longer believe that God is not only loving but also ultimately victorious. As Barth preached the triumph of God in Easter, guns boomed in the distance, signaling the frustration, the doom, and the lie of any possibility of human triumph. The historical, largely unmentioned context of this sermon therefore makes the triumphant message of this sermon all the more gripping and poignant.

April 29, 1917

2 Peter 3:12a

Wait for and hasten to the coming of the day of God! (alt.; cf. German)

Dear friends!

"Wait for and hasten to!" A Word spoken as if straight from the heart of the Bible! In it one hears a festive sound and song, inviting and promising. It also contains something majestic and sublime, almost unapproachable, a jubilation as if sung by angel choirs, the sound of rushing as if from underground springs, a great rumble as if from a far-off thunderstorm. It is something so oddly clear and revealing, but then again enigmatic, mysterious, concealing, as when a lightning bolt lightens the whole landscape only to leave it again in darkness, or when a curtain goes up only to fall again, or when a voice speaks out clearly and in a friendly way, but in a foreign language. A Word spoken out of the Spirit of God. And therefore, dear friends, the Spirit, the Holy Spirit of God, must open our ears so that we may hear what the Word has to say to us.

"Wait for and hasten to!" That is the answer of the Bible to a human question. The question itself stands in the Bible, and in more than one place. The question is, "What shall we do?" [e.g., Luke 3:10, 12, 14; Acts 2:37]. This is the question one asks when one once realizes that one should do something other than the usual. It is the question, for example, of the rich man when the meaning of his wealth and situation of comfortable well-being becomes questionable, when his money and beautiful home have become uncomfortable to the point of being a little sinister. It is the question of the young woman when she becomes aware that nice clothes and marriage are not the total of what a young

25

woman should think about. It is the question of the pastor when his position and peculiar dignity in the midst of worldly life strike him as odd. It is the question of superficial persons when they become anxious about their soul. It is the question of the philanthropists, who are full of good will, when they realize how little help one can really give human beings. It is the question of the politician when in quiet hours his political skill strikes him as suspect. It is the question of the business man when he is not fully satisfied with what he is doing, but is driven now and again by a mysterious disquiet, so that he glances down with the question, "Where have I come from, and where am I really going?" It is the question of the housewife to whom all those small but important things she does are not as meaningful as they once were. It is the question of pious persons who have been, so to speak, tapped on the shoulder and no longer enjoy a completely peaceful sleep in their quiet homes. All of them ask, "What should we do?" The answer of the Bible is, "Wait for and hasten to!" It is valid for each of us, just as at bottom the question is asked by all of us.

There is in us all a kind of track, like a railroad track, onto which we have been rolled and on which we are still rolling. We all know of our own holy rightfulness, a right on which we rely and which we spread out before us like a carefully written and advantageous bank statement. For one person this holy right is called "my character!" For another, "my view of life, which is naturally in unison with that of all good and right people!" For another, "what I have learned from experience!" For another, "my Christianity!" or "my views in important matters!" or "my politics, all thought out in my own head!" For another it is called "my family" or "my husband" or "my brother," and for yet another it may be only "me myself: I am of course important and I rightfully place myself above all others."—Look well: this track on which we are rolling, this holy right on which we rely, is a human being, and with the human each of us is well acquainted.

But each of us also knows that *there is something* in the world that protests against the human being and its right, something that puts us all in question by asking about the real meaning of the "you" and "yours," and, so to speak, by striking though our neatly done arithmetic like a teacher who has found it wrong. There is an experience that ruins all our other experiences; there is an insight that causes our previous view of things to be thrown out; there is a kind of wake-up call that intends energetically to wake us from the sleep we have been sleeping till now. There is something in us that wants to shake us up and throw us off our usual track, a voice that calls, whether loudly or softly, "You should not just keep rolling like a railroad car on your accustomed track! You are not a railroad car, you are a living person, and you must be your own mover and move yourself!"—And if we then, still dull with sleep, do get about the business of doing something in response to this voice, it will be half joyful and half in dread, partly convinced that something has to change and yet partly clinging to the old, holy right that we do not want to let go. Then a question emerges, as if it just popped up by itself, a question that wants an answer and yet is also rather peevish and defensive: "What am I really supposed to do?"

To this very human question the Bible gives this *answer*: "Wait for and hasten to the coming of the day of God!" Indeed, the Bible often gives our remarkable questions remarkable answers.

What is really the *human being*, with its own holy right—which, as we have said, all of us are well acquainted with? How is it *possible* that we all have rolled like rail cars so happily and securely on our different tracks, and perhaps still do? What drives human beings so actively and persistently such as, for example, people from all the world to the business center of Zurich? What makes a young lad so impudent and fresh? the pastor so solemn and officious? the members of a political party so agitated and quarrelsome? men so proud and self-conscious? women so attentive and sensible? superficial persons so amusing, and pious persons so strict and serious? What makes a human being just a human being, each with one's own small—or rather infinitely important—"I myself, my own." It all comes from one astonishing source: we all belong to God! We all have something of God in us: a part, a splinter, a beam of God's light, a branch torn from the tree of life. God is with all of us, and for God, each of us is right. I say that unambiguously: for God, each of us is right. Our own holy right is really a piece of the righteousness of God.

Whoever we are and however we live, God says to each of us not "No," but "Yes!" God says "Yes" to the laughter of amusing people and to the crying of those who are in sorrow; to the quiet work of the farmer working in his acre; to the busy cleaning and ordering of the housewife; to the accounting of the merchant; to the studiousness of the pastor; to the watchfulness of the soldier at his post. God says "Yes" to very different persons: to those who can take life lightly and live happily, and to those who drag themselves and life from place to place with heavy sighs; to those who are gentle and mild, and to those who are agitated and passionate; to those who are able to handle any situation, and to those who constantly protest and have to defend themselves.

Over all and for all, the great and patient "Yes!" of God is spoken. "Yes, you may and you should be just what you are." God says "Yes!" even when we confront one another with our different views and standpoints: human being may judge us wrong, but before God, remarkably, we are always right. You wish to be Catholic? You may. You are a *socialist*? That you may be. In your heart you burn for the nation, the "fatherland"? That too you may do. Are you dedicated to abstinence? to a pietist community? to a cooperative program? That is what is wonderful: that for God we may do all of these things; that each may be oneself; that each may express oneself like children at play; that each may run one's own course. Everywhere something of God's righteousness runs along with us.

We would not be so passionate, so self-conscious, so sure, if we did not belong to God. Even all the security and surety with which we keep rolling on our accustomed tracks is something we have from God. We could not be so fresh, so hotheaded, so hard, so quarrelsome, and behave so badly without this divine right that runs with us on all our personal ways. The whole fervor too with which we say "I!" and "mine!" comes actually out of the memory that I belong to God!

Certainly *something evil can* happen and has happened in us, when we speak and hear about this truth. It is *God* who says to us in such a friendly way and so patiently: "Yes, you may and should be what you are." But when we hear this "Yes" and accept it, and then push God *aside*, that is when it turns to evil. How sad it is that precisely *this* is what we ever again do! How sad that we want, without God, to assume this right to be what we are. What a pity that we smash this God-given vessel and run on with a mere shard in our hand, instead of living with the whole! What a pity that we, like foolish boys, break the limb from the tree, with the result that it withers! Now the truth turns into a lie. Our music sounds off-key: "I!" and "mine!"—without God. Now our right becomes empty—without God! We become such ridiculous little railcars, instead of living beings—without God! Our opinions and points of view protrude so uselessly, like the ruins of an ancient robber baron's fortress. So poisonously do our different characters collide. So devoid of understanding and with such hostility do those who belong to one social class, one political party, or one religion pass by those of another social class, political party, or religion.

Such dreadful confusion have human beings themselves caused, with the result of world war—only because we do not want to hear and understand that we may go our ways *with God*, that God wants to be *with us* as we go our ways. This is the evil day of humanity, this confusion, which began with the fall into sin of the first human being. That human being wanted to be like God [cf. Gen. 3:5]—without God, against God. It is no wonder that we cannot remain calm and secure in this confusion. It is impossible, in spite of the great and patient "Yes!" that God has spoken over all of us, in spite of God's divine right that everywhere and with each of us runs a little along with us. We do not accept it from God; instead, we want to seize it for ourselves. That is why we must be in hell and torment [cf. Luke 16:23].

From time to time a thick line is drawn through our arithmetic, clearly showing that it is wrong; we become aware of what it means to run along one's way without God, and that we are in hell and torment. We are shaken by a shaking that wants to throw us off the dead track: the war, the revolution in Russia, the precious time we have left, the death that now and again enters a house, the nagging disquiet in one's conscience, the silent discord in many families, the emptiness in so many lives that leaves none satisfied, and the awareness that all this should not continue among the peoples of the earth! It knocks at the door, calls, speaks, and gives us no rest. What is all of this? Look again: how remarkable—here again is God! God, who certainly must now say to us not "Yes!" but "No!" We cannot escape the fact that we belong to God. God never lets us leave God.

If we have misused God's goodness, then we must experience God's judgment, and yet God's grace is in both. That is why the thought has seized upon some happy and distinguished people—such as Francis of Assisi in his youth and Count Tolstoy shortly before his death—that they must put everything behind them in order to get away from their wealth and situation of comfortable well-being. *That is why* there are ever again persons who, without having especially bad deeds on their consciences, all at once cry out in their souls: "Wretched person that I am! Who will rescue me from this body of death?" [Rom. 7:24], and in torment want to change fundamentally, to convert. *That is why* there are socialists and anarchists who are discontented with everything and want to bring down all that stands. *That is why* many pastors today are no longer the peaceful men of the church and friends of everyone, like pastors were fifty years ago. *That is why* there burns in all of us such a hot, unquenchable restlessness and longing for something better.

But that is also why we cannot get away from it all, why all this *has to be*, because the heavy line through our arithmetic, the shaking, the question mark over our whole being comes not by chance but from

God. It is as if we were compelled not to feel at home in *the* world that is abandoned by God, but must desire that other lost world. God moves in a restless conscience and in a head full of stirred-up thoughts. God grumbles in the discontented masses, sighs in the millions of those who weep, and is angry in the thousands who know how things are. As God has given us all our rightfulness, so also do we all feel, necessarily, the divine protest, the divine accusation and threatening. When one looks out of hate-filled eyes, God looks out of these eyes too; when fists are made, God is with these fists. Swords are sharpened, and God will know how to use them. That is the other side of the truth: the judgment, the divine "No," the shaking, and perhaps the ruin and destruction, that threatens our whole being.

We can also *misunderstand* this side of the truth, and we have misunderstood it a thousand times. We can hear the divine "No" and yet not want to hear God. Here too we can seize for ourselves what belongs to God and pass God by. Here too the human being can take the upper hand and occupy the center of the stage. We can even give away and sacrifice everything, ourselves too—without God! We can want to change ourselves from the ground up and convert, only not to God! We can grumble with the discontented, scold, make fists, destroy, but without God! We can be consumed by the pain of our conscience and by the desire for what is better, and remain at a great distance from God. Then the confusion becomes vexation, the day of human beings becomes darker and darker, hell ever more terrible, judgment ever more severe.

What should we do? This question, which is *the question* of human beings, stands again before us. We know now from whence it comes. We stand under the patience of God and under the judgment of God; and we have failed to recognize, have not wanted to recognize, God in either, in both. At one time we only want to hear the "Yes" and so to be what we are, but not in and with God. At another time we only want to hear the "No" and to renew and change ourselves, but without becoming new in God, without beginning anew with God. What should we do? Yes, what should we do, when we do not want to do the one thing that we should do? We know what is to be done: "Wait for and hasten to the coming day of the Lord."

The *day of God* is the day when God will be acknowledged as right—the same patient and passionate God that we ever again refuse to understand. That will be the day when God will bless us through his goodness and purify us through his judgment. That will be the day when we hear both from *God's own* mouth: both the "Yes," with which God gives us our right to be what we are, and the "No," with which God puts away our falseness, all that is wrong, and consumes it with fire [cf. 2. Pet. 3:12b]. It will be the day of salvation from our confusions and the day of the end of our restless disquiet.

Will the evil day of human beings ever end? "Wait for and hasten to the coming day of the Lord." Give God the honor! Place yourselves on *God's* side! Not *you* are what is important—neither what you are nor what you become, but *God*, what *God* is and will do through you! Hear both: the word of God's unending patience [cf. 2 Pet. 3:9, 15] and the word of God's consuming passion [Zeph. 1:18; 3:8]—only hear them as *God's* Word. What should we do? The day of God brings the answer, God is the answer. Let us only take care that we are able to hear it.

Amen.

COMMENTS

What are we supposed to do? The answer from the "heart of the Bible"? "Wait for and hasten to." Barth loves antitheses: hurry up and wait! "We tarry and—hurry" appears in more than one place in *Romans* (30, 33). He is very much in a paradoxical frame of mind. The preacher is struggling with how to bring the complexities of a true and living God to speech, attempting, it would seem, to help the congregation learn how to think in a whole new way. He admits up front that this biblical thought is "almost unapproachable." Only paradoxical thinking and dialectical rhetoric can do justice to the inherently paradoxical quality of the gospel. Our speech must match the odd truth of the gospel, whose message is "enigmatic, mysterious, concealing, as when a lightning bolt lightens the whole landscape only to leave it again in darkness." Claims that we are owned and loved by God are placed alongside our rebellion against God. The day of the Lord is both our mercy and our judgment at the same time.

"What is really the *human being*?" asks the young preacher, a question that the mature Barth would rarely ask or, if asked, would give a quite different answer than the one he gives in this sermon. "We all have something of God in us: a part, a splinter, a beam of God's light, a branch torn from the tree of life. God is with all of us," claims the preacher, thus establishing a point of contact between gospel and congregation. In *Romans* Barth declared the complete independence of revelation. There is a great difference between our knowledge of God and our knowledge of all creaturely reality. In these sermons it is as if Barth is teaching his congregation a new way of thinking.

To better understand what the preacher is attempting here, we need a short excursus on Wilhelm Herrmann (1846–1922), the chief theological mentor of both Barth and Bultmann.[1] From Herrmann, Barth received his notion of the complete independence, the inherent oddness of religion. There is no grounding of faith other than the grounding that is given by God in the individual's encounter with God. God is not some entity that is generally available to us by our means of making sense of the world. Most of us preachers were taught to study the Bible by would-be historians. Herrmann said that was a mistake. The methods of history cannot lead to the truth that is Jesus Christ.

The liberal "inner Jesus" of Herrmann seemed to the young Barth to be a most credible basis for the Christian faith to make its way with the modern world. There was widespread agreement in German theological circles that the search for a "Jesus of history" had ended in a dead end. The century of attempts at a historical reconstruction of Jesus rendered a Jesus who looked suspiciously like a mirror image of the historians themselves. Furthermore, the various portraits of the "historical Jesus" that had been devised were extremely thin and decidedly opposed to the Jesus who was worshiped by the church. After rummaging about in the remains of the historical Jesus, historians had not left modern people with much of a Jesus in whom to believe.

Herrmann's answer in *The Communion of the Christian with God* was to turn from a historical Jesus toward a subjective, "inner Jesus." From Herrmann, Barth learned to be suspicious of historical Jesus reconstruction efforts as the attempt to step outside of faith into some supposedly objective security provided by historical research. Faith cannot be defended or justified by some means external to the faith itself, said Herrmann. Historical research into Scripture can therefore play an important but only secondary role when thinking about Jesus. Thinking about Jesus requires a peculiar kind of inner, subjective appropriation of Jesus that mere historical thinking cannot muster.

The unknowable God can only be known if God makes God's self known. Knowledge of God is not something produced by the forces of history. An act of God is required. The important thing is a believer's individual experience with Christ, an experience that the liberal assumes is on a rather comfortable continuum between the believer and Christ. In Jesus Christ unintuitable God graciously becomes intuitable to the believer. The truth claims of theology cannot be grounded in historical data; they can only be grounded in subjective intuition, a gift of a God who always refuses to be hidden from us.

Herrmann owed a great debt to Schleiermacher. We ought not trouble ourselves over finding some unassailable historical core to Jesus, said Herrmann. Modern historical criticism's inability to recover much factual evidence of Jesus is only a threat to faith when we misunderstand faith. We are not saved by faith in historical information about Jesus but rather by the very person of Jesus as we encounter him and experience him. As our inner beings encounter the inner essence of Christ, we shall be changed by that encounter.

Talk of this sort is certainly reminiscent of Pietism. Rebirth, regeneration is the necessary precondition of all knowledge that is truly theological knowledge. Herrmann saw himself as a theologian who breathed new life into Luther's justification by faith alone as opposed to all dry creedalism and dead legalism. The Bible is "true" and authoritative solely on the basis of its ability accurately to describe what it is like to be encountered by Christ. The Bible is God's word solely in its capacity to bring people into communion with God. Thus Barth said that faith is not comprehension, grasping, or intellectual understanding. Faith is "motionless, silence, worship . . . not-knowing" (202). Faith is "a leap into the darkness of the unknown, a flight into empty air" (98).

Christian truth is elusive, subtle truth, a "secret in the soul" that cannot be handed over from one person to another. It is up to God, working in our innermost selves, to enliven and provoke faith. Faith as an engaging, inner encounter with the living Christ is the only means whereby we have communion with God. "The thoughts of others who are redeemed cannot redeem me," said Herrmann. Nothing can be called "revelation" until it acts upon me to bring me into communion with God. Christianity is not a set of abstract intellectual propositions; it is an event of faith and relationship to Christ.

Barth's April 29, 1917, sermon shows both an indebtedness to Herrmann as well as the beginnings of a struggle against him. Herrmann tended to drive a wedge between the inner life of Jesus and the actual works and words of Jesus in the Gospels. The content of Jesus' message had less import than the encounter with Jesus. Thus Herrmann fostered agnosticism about the historical content of Jesus combined with great faith in the subjective, individual appropriation of Jesus.

Although Herrmann insisted that this was not religious subjectivism, it was difficult to maintain the objective reality of God in all this talk of secrets in the soul and inner appropriation of Jesus. Though Herrmann kept referring to Jesus as a "fact," it was difficult to find the facts in all this. His "inner Jesus" was a Jesus without much content. Much of the specific substance of Christ, including his ethical claims, seemed to blur and fade as everything about Jesus was subsumed into the dramatic, life-changing existential "encounter" with Christ.

Rudolf Bultmann said that *Romans* could be summed up as an assertion of "*the independence and the absolute nature of religion*."[2] The thought is vintage Herrmann. Thinking about religious matters requires a very different sort of thinking. In thinking thus, Herrmann was one of the most notable in a long train of nineteenth-century attempts to rescue the Christian faith from the ravages of modern criticism, to preserve something of Christ that was worthy of our belief, a process that began at least with Schleiermacher. In Schleiermachian fashion, Herrmann removed faith from the withering gaze of science and history by moving it into subjective experience. Barth later recalled his thrill at hearing Herrmann's critique of modern attempts at historical retrieval of Jesus. The seminarian also resonated with Herrmann's refusal to do apologetics: when faith comes to someone, it comes as a gift of God, not as a result of well-reasoned arguments. The preacher must present the gospel "without weapons," without relying on any philosophical arguments, historical proofs, or rational demonstrations. These themes continued in Barth's later thought, but with his distinctive appropriation of them. Barth would continue later, in the *Church Dogmatics*, find it necessary to overcome Herrmann's psychologism, even as Herrmann had tried to overcome the historicism of the nineteenth century.

I wonder if Herrmann is partly responsible for this sermon's rather abstract quality. The preacher warns us that this sermon is based upon a text as a voice that "speaks out clearly and in a friendly way, but in a foreign language." Still, the preacher comes perilously close to making the "day of the Lord" into a psychological experience. The day of the Lord is that current moment whenever God comes close to us and, in coming close, utterly changes us. Changed into what? The sermon is thus an early example of the sort of presentation of the gospel that George Lindbeck (in *The Nature of Doctrine*) called "experiential/expressive." What is religion? The liberal theologian answers that religion is a universal phenomenon that expresses, in varying, albeit primitive ways, the deepest or most exalted aspirations of humanity's search for God. To put it bluntly, our religious thoughts arise from within us and move toward God. Later Barth stressed that such religious sentiments and aspirations are nothing less than idolatry, the attempt to fashion a "god" in our own image. God comes to us as God is and resists all our attempts to make God over into a divinity more compatible with our humanity. This sermon tends to be more experimental and experiential than scriptural. In the end it implies that our experience of God validates God.

In 1917 Rudolf Otto (1869–1937) published *The Idea of the Holy* (in Germany), a romantic presentation of the Christian faith, wholly without interest in historical issues. God, whom Otto called the "wholly other," has no place in our scheme of reality. The "trembling soul" stands in awe before the *mysterium tremendum.* "The kingdom of God, as already at hand, is . . . the inbreaking miraculous power of the transcendent."

Here is Barth, indebted to Otto and to Herrmann, still the enthusiastic young liberal, the committed student of Herrmann who seeks to present the gospel "in rigorously individual terms," and yet one has the impression that Barth cannot fully square his experiential liberalism with Scripture. Perhaps that is why the notion of the "day of the Lord" just seems to hover above this sermon, hanging there undefined, unexplored, without much substantive content, without real relationship to this need for us to "hurry up and wait."

If this sermon sounds familiar to us, even with its now-strange existentialist approach or its paradoxical and dialectical language, it is because this is the sermon form that has been utilized by most of us North American preachers for the past fifty years. The preacher begins with an assessment of the "human condition," then after having rummaged about in Scripture for some text that allegedly speaks to the problems raised by the preacher's characterization of the human condition, presents that as a biblical "answer" to current human "questions." First practiced by theological liberals in Germany, then wholeheartedly embraced by Protestant mainline preachers in the United States after Harry Emerson Fosdick, this has become a favorite sermon form for so-called evangelicals like Rick Warren or Joel Osteen. We're all nineteenth-century German liberals now.

In just a couple of years Barth came to see Herrmann's work as a kind of academic concoction pitched mainly to the faith struggles of fellow intellectuals, irrelevant either to the gospel or to the Safenwilers. By the time he wrote *Romans,* he proclaimed that "human experience and human perception end where God begins" (120).

January 27, 1918 (Leutwil);
February 3, 1918 (Safenwil)

Luke 3:21–22

Now when the people were baptized, and when Jesus also had been baptized and was praying, the heaven was opened, and the Holy Spirit descended upon him in bodily form like a dove. And a voice came from heaven, "You are my Son, the Beloved; with you I am well pleased."

Dear friends!

Truthfully all of us wish that God would be well pleased with us— not only good and pious persons, but also the bad and the unbelieving; indeed, these more than ever wish it, and often far stronger than the good and pious. There is simply that in a human being that wants and waits to hear such a voice, a voice that would say to oneself, "With you I am well pleased!" As different as they otherwise may be, in this respect all people are alike. And perhaps their differences only come from the different ways they all want the same thing, strive for the same goal. Yes, God's good pleasure is like a sea into which all streams and rivers flow.

We remember Christmas and the angels singing of God's good pleasure on the night of Christ's birth. And it would be God's good pleasure, if God were now to say to you: "To me you are just right the way you are! I acknowledge you, I like you! Now be and remain what you are and the way you are, for you are good and right!" That would be something wonderful, would it not? Imagine that—just as there was once such a person on the Jordan with John the Baptist—there were also someone here in the church to whom God could say those same words. Imagine that we would know who this person is. Would we not feel remarkably blessed by this person's presence? Would we not feel how one such person could be a blessing for a whole village and region, and how much we today actually have no greater need than for a few persons here and there with whom God is well pleased?

We are indeed aware that, if someone were present among us to whom God could say, "I like you just as you are!" there would be something like a glow around that one, and we would feel strangely well in being near them. All kinds of things would be possible that otherwise seem impossible, and so many things that we would be better off without would disappear. There would emanate from this person something like a power to dry tears, a power to turn hostile faces into friendly faces and hard hands into open hands, a power to disperse bad thoughts and do other wonders. That would be a great event: to have such a person, a person well pleasing to God, in our midst. It would be the greatest event we could possibly experience.

And now imagine what seems even more inconceivable: imagine that one of us were allowed to listen to what is transpiring in one's own soul, and instead of the many wild, agitated, restless voices we usually hear, one would hear, in all its strength and tranquility, that one voice that came from heaven and was heard on the Jordan. Imagine that this single person among us would hear the words spoken about oneself: "With you I am well pleased!" Oh, we all wish so much to be acknowledged and approved by others. When anyone says we are right, it gives us a good feeling. We conduct so many conversations with the quiet and shy intention of receiving perhaps a little praise from the other, of hearing perhaps just a little of that wonderful sound: "Be and remain just as you are, for that is good and right!"

If we could just once hear those words with complete, unconditioned certainty—not only from another person, who perhaps might later say the opposite, but spoken as it were from the very foundation of the world with a deep and unshakable surety—then we could no longer doubt: "It is good and right that you are as you are!" Yes, we would give a lot to hear that. Every human being hungers and thirsts for that more than for food and drink. It is one of the very deep and hot wishes that each of us has within.

Whoever did hear it would be full of an indescribable, incomparable joy and become a new kind of person. One would be able all at once to be friendly to difficult people, patiently to bear the heavy burdens of life, courageously to resist strong and intense temptations, to be kind to everyone—and all that not as something unusual that one would have to work oneself up to, but as something natural and something that could not be otherwise. Through all difficulties and obstacles it would have to be carried within in deep awareness: "Come what may, I know that I am right and that I may and should be just as I am." There is no greater power that can ever come to a person than this clarity and certainty.

Dear friends, that is the clarity and certainty that the Savior had and that we can neither imitate nor seize for ourselves. We must rather leave it entirely to him, for it was and is something that belonged and belongs only to him. It is important that we read this about him: the heaven was opened above him, a heavenly voice was audible, and something was especially remarkable: the Holy Spirit descended upon him in physical form, like a dove. We can see that, when a human being is the recipient of God's good pleasure, it really is a miracle, an entirely extraordinary revelation of a higher world. It is not something that just happens by itself; no human being can be reared or educated into receiving it. No degree of effort can accomplish it, and there is no possible way to obtain it. If it ever comes to us, it does so only as a gift and as something completely new and unheard of on earth.

In distinction from all other great and pious persons, of whom we are told or read how they progressively accomplished great things, we hear nothing about how the Savior came to know and to be obedient to God, to be converted to God, to love human beings, to gain God's good pleasure. Rather, we simply hear that something was within him from the beginning that we from the beginning do not have. It is said of him that he "increased in divine and human favor" [Luke 2:52]. That "something" grew, like a flower grows or as fruit ripens. In order that something grow and ripen, it must have a seed within it. That was the miracle: the divine, the heavenly within the Savior, and not that he was reared well, not that he was a serious and pious child who tried hard and dwelled in serious thoughts. He might have been and done all that too, but what was most important was, from the beginning, a seed within him, a seed of grace and God's good pleasure, a small voice that spoke softly to him, "You are right; be and remain as you are!"

As a child of twelve he had already said, as something entirely natural for him: "I must be in my Father's house" [Luke 2:49]. This good pleasure was said of his speaking before he opened his mouth to speak, of his hands before he stretched them out to do something, of his steps before he went here and there. It stood behind him and it went before him. It was the home from which he went out and into which he ever again returned. It was the source of his life. Because such a divine good pleasure was upon him, he could become what he became.

All the words of the Savior that have so wonderfully shined, like heavenly stars, and that still shine today for those who can see them;

all the deeds of the Savior with which he reached deeply into human distress and showed us that there is something other than the curse of sin and death under which we still suffer; the exceedingly great victory in which he, on the cross, finally broke through the prison walls of the present human world—all flowed from this one source: that he was well pleasing to God. For there is nothing stronger and greater. It is light in darkness and help in weakness, it is victory and overcoming in our sins and cares and perplexities when God can say to a person: "You are right; you must be as you are. I wish to have you just as you are!"

That is what we are lacking. All of us are driven by the disquieting sense that we should be different. We are all plagued and even crippled by the awareness that, as we are, we can find no acceptance and approval; and we consume our energy in a struggle with ourselves, in vain endeavors to make ourselves different. Meanwhile life goes on, and we are not able to answer its questions or do its tasks. Everything stands against us like rough blocks and boulders: sin, fate, Mammon, war, mortality, and above all that vain and simple wretch that looks back at us in the mirror. Not we are the masters, but these blocks and boulders. It is not we who rule them, but they us. They crush us, and we are completely subjected to them.

That is why life seems so difficult, and just *how* difficult life is becomes clearer every day. It is a burden none of us is able to lift. Why not? Because we are not right. We all would very much like to be right, and people do often say we are right, and we are glad of it. But we know very well that for God we are not right. If God could approve of us and praise us, then we would know for the first time how free and strong the human being was created to be, know the kinds of power that sleep inertly within us, know how much all the things we experience within could be and must be dependent on the power of the Spirit. If God were for us, who would be against us? [Rom. 8:31]. If we were sure that God does not oppose us but rather stands behind us and gives us strength, what burdens could we not then lift and carry? If within us we had the clarity and certainty that, just as we are, we may go forward with God, what could hang over us and cause fear, as do the thousand dangers, temptations, and cares now hanging over us? In our present state these dangers, temptations, and cares are like that sharp sword that hung by a thread over the head of ancient King Damocles. This is where we are lacking!

But not the Savior. We are surely quite correct in thinking that God does not find us well pleasing. The Savior knew that God's good pleasure was with him. What for us is the most inconceivable, that was for him entirely natural. What for us is the last, most beautiful goal of our life, that for which we work and wrestle, all the while falling into so many errors—that was for him in good order when he began his life. It was for him the air he breathed. That is why the Savior is for us ever again so wonderful in all he said and did, such a heavenly appearance in the human world: because we feel and know that from the beginning he had something that we do not have.

That is why too the biblical story of his baptism is a genuine miracle story. For it was and is for us a miracle, something new, completely unusual and surprising, that there was once a human being who quietly grew up in the grace and good pleasure of God, and who then stepped out into adult life with this power behind him and in him. It is astonishing, still today as it was then, that a human being, like we are, lived and was nourished from a source that is still almost completely unknown and almost fully closed to us. Compared with this nourishment, the outward sign that came from heaven is less astonishing. But how could it have been otherwise? Where the earth was blessed once again from heaven, how could there not also be something seen and heard from heaven?

How it is possible that the divine good pleasure, with all its powerful effects, could be with a human being on this old earth in this way? And what does it mean for us, who have to continue to live on this old earth? The other words of the text give us the answer; they show the meaning and consequence: "You are my Son, the Beloved!" There we have it! How should God not be joyful about what comes from God, not bless the one who has his origin in God, not find him right, whom God has made right? What God does, is done well. God saw what God had made, and God saw that it was good [Gen. 1:31]. God saw the Savior as in a mirror, and so God saw in him no stranger, but God's own image. It is like a human father seeing his son, finding his own features in his face, rejoicing that he has the son, acknowledging him, giving him all his love, and helping him as well as he can, from the beginning, simply because he is his son! That is Jesus' secret: he comes from God!

When we look at ourselves, we have to say: We are what the family in which we were born has made us; we are what the education that we enjoyed and the social conditions in which we grew up have made us; we are what good and bad influences have made us—and we affirm all this as our personal history. Somehow we too come from God, have our origin in God, but so much has come between us and God. And if one considers us on the whole, one may have the impression with us too, in some small way, that "what God does, is well done," although in regard to many, very many human beings one rather thinks: "Oh, what a noble spirit has here been destroyed," and "Once again the thoughts and intentions of God have been ruined." In any case, however, when God looks at us, God does not see God's own mirror image, but a stranger, a being that has become completely unlike God. The divine origin in us is concealed, buried, and forgotten.

That is why God's good pleasure cannot be with us; God can rejoice only in one who comes from God. And we must bear the consequences: Where God has no joy, there we too can have none. If *God* does not say we are right, we are not right. If *God* does not hold us, we have nothing to hold on to. That is why we are always lacking what is most important. Jesus came from God, like a second, new creation of human being. It was as if God wanted to say: "I can no longer stand seeing nothing but strange faces on earth; and you human children also cannot stand it, as oppressed and imprisoned as you are, because you have become strangers to me. I can no longer hold back my good pleasure, for I so much want it in a human being. From now on there shall be no more talk of all the emptiness, sadness, and foolishness that separate you from me. Now in a human being the doors shall again open, so that you may see who you truly are. Away with all that is twisted, artificial, and untruthful! Here you have one who shall tell you and show you that the human being belongs to God!"

God has given us Jesus Christ, his beloved Son, and he stands before us as a human being—yes, in all respects he was found as a human being, as one of us [cf. Phil. 2:7]. Yet he was a human being who did not have a strange face for God, but the face of a child in the eyes of its father. In him the deepest and best was not buried and forgotten but emerged openly into the light of day. With him one did not have the doubt that he could be too closely related to the animal. Rather, with him one could again, finally, at long last, see, hear, and touch something of our eternal, divine origin, the Son of the Father, full of grace and truth [John 1:14]. And here could God's good pleasure finally break into this world again, the good pleasure that God had long wished to have with human beings and that God would like to have with us— indeed God would like nothing more than this! In the life of the Savior we see what kind of inbreaking into our world it was, for in him we see a great light, great power, help, and liberation.

"You are my Son, the Beloved!" It is true, is it not, that we understand that these words cannot have to do only with the Savior, but that what God says to him, God says to us all. God says it to him so that we may all hear again how very important the Savior is for us. The Savior stands in the bright light of God's good pleasure, as the human being that God says is right and whom he helps; but the Savior will not stand alone: we should all stand where he stands. What he was then, the blessed Son of the Father, there on the Jordan 2,000 years ago, he will not be only for himself. His will is to be the firstborn of many brothers and sisters [cf. Rom. 8:29].

We are the brothers and sisters. We regard him today from a distance, and we think, with thoughts both melancholy and envious, of how good we could have it in the Father's house. It is so very unnecessary that we should stand to the side and think, "Yes, there is the Savior, and here we are, far away from him." No, we must only see him rightly, and then we will also see who we ourselves really are. When that happens, there will awaken also in us that other, deeper reality, and our origin as human beings will break in upon us again too. The Savior will become for us a mirror in which we may see ourselves. And if we learn to look deeply into this mirror, then we may realize that we belong to God and hear God speaking to us, "You are my beloved children!" Then we may know and feel that God will bless us all and make it well with us all.

The Savior is the beginning of a new creation of God on this old, dark earth, and God wants this new creation to go farther and include us too. When we are included, God's good pleasure will no longer be something distant. We cannot imitate the flower and fruit that grew and ripened from that divine seed in the Savior, but when we once hear the words, "You are my Son, the Beloved! You, the Savior, are the divine seed!" then there will be a growing and ripening in us too, and we will marvel at it.

Amen.

COMMENTS

Barth begins his sermon on the baptism of Jesus in a surprising way—surprising to those of us who know something of Barthian theological commitments. He begins the sermon with us, with our longing "that God would be well pleased with us." While I wonder if Barth exaggerates the universality of this human desire for divine good pleasure, he is surely right that the pious and the impious long to hear God murmur to us sweetly, "To me you are just right the way you are! I acknowledge you, I like you! Now be and remain what you are and the way you are, for you are good and right!" Joel Osteen could not have said it with more syrup. Imagine how wonderful it would be to be in the presence of a human being who was able to say, "Come what may, I know that I am right and that I may and should be just as I am."

This first fourth of the sermon is surely a sly preacher ploy. Barth lures us in with sweet talk of divine approval only to flip the sermon back upon us with the jolting assertion that none of this applies to us. In *Romans,* Barth declares that we must never "confuse grace with human possibility" (214). Grace is not what we do or feel; "grace means that God does something" (215). Baptism is clearly depicted here as signifying, displaying that miraculous work.

The preacher reminds us that the text is a description of the baptism of Jesus, not of us. The words of God's complete, well-pleased commendation were spoken only to Jesus, not to us. While Barth flirts with Adoptionism in his comments about Jesus' growing awareness of divine approval, the sermon here makes a sharp turn from anthropology to theology. In this text we are given the privilege of listening in on miraculous words from "a higher world." The baptismal voice signifies that this one "comes from God." Only Jesus is addressed in this way in his baptism. Only Jesus had no need to develop into a better person. Jesus is the only one among us to whom God could say without reservation, "I am well pleased with you."

This sense of divine approval, this miraculous holy attestation, is what "we are lacking!" And yet the one who stands in Jordan water in solidarity with sinners is also a sign that, in our lack and deprivation, we are not lacking God's presence. Jesus' baptism is not only sign of his exalted divinity but also of his close-by humanity. In observing his baptism we have a hint that "somehow we too come from God, have our origin in God," even though "so much has come between us and God."

Having affirmed our lack, our need for improvement, our distance from God; having testified to the divine nature of Jesus and his radical distance from us, Barth then makes a surprising turn in stressing the nearness of Jesus to us: "These words cannot have to do only with the Savior, but that what God says to him, God says to us all. God says it to him so that we may all hear again how very important the Savior is for us. The Savior stands in the bright light of God's good pleasure, as the human being that God says is right and whom he helps; but the Savior will not stand alone: we should all stand where he stands." Because "he will not stand alone," Jesus is sign of our divine adoption. The divine Son of God has made us nothing less than his "brothers and sisters."

Barth, who became notorious in *Romans* for his Kierkegaardian stress upon the "infinite qualitative distance" between God and humanity, says toward the end of the sermon that we make a big mistake to fixate on the distance between God and humanity. There is a distance, but that gulf has been bridged by God in Jesus Christ. The voice that speaks at Jesus' baptism speaks to us, and it is the voice of God with us. Thus, when we "see him rightly, . . . then we will also see who we ourselves really are." Who are we? We are not only those in a sorry state; we are those who marvel to have been encountered, embraced in the Son, with whom the Father is well pleased. As Barth said in *Romans*, "Truth is not what we say about God, but what He does and will do and has done" (301).

This sermon goes somewhere, making two or three interesting twists and turns arising out of, and referring us back to, the biblical text. In its movement from earth to heaven, then definitively back to earth, it displays some of the theology of the incarnation described in narrative form in the text itself. The sermon begins with a rather conventional assessment of the human situation, but it has no intention of leaving us there. Rather, it moves from anthropology to Christology and thereby ends up with something really interesting to say.

Many lessons for us contemporary preachers are to be learned here.

March 3, 1918

Romans 12:1–2

> I appeal to you therefore, brothers and sisters, by the mercies of God, to present your bodies as a living sacrifice, holy and well pleasing to God, which is your reasonable worship.[1] Do not be conformed to this world, but be transformed by the renewing of your minds, so that you may discern what is the will of God—what is good and acceptable and perfect.

Dear friends!

With these words the apostle Paul leads us again into that holy place *before which* we have often silently stood, astonished and full of wonder, and yet rather estranged and disconcerted. When we consider the words of the Bible with only a little real attention and, as it were, from within it, they all have more or less the effect of leading us to the point where we do not rightly know whether we should rejoice or sigh, whether we should grasp them with both hands or draw back in hesitation. On all its pages and especially in the New Testament, the Bible is a book that very strongly and very clearly offers us something about which we must decide. It asks us a question to which we must answer yes or no. We recognize that, if we say yes, it would be something great and glorious; but we also notice that saying yes would be of great consequence, for it would have a huge effect on the way we live.

Indeed, it must strike us as almost uncanny to think about saying yes to something that would then penetrate so deeply into our thoughts, opinions, and decisions. For this reason we hesitate, and in our hesitation we reverse the question. While *we* should answer the question that is asked of *us*, we now ask the question: "Is this truly something for me? Can I understand it, and am I able really to enter into it? Can a person of our time enter into it at all? And if we really do risk it, what happens to our wishes, our concerns, our pain?"

Our text leads us to this remarkable point, where we should be the ones to give answer, but where we ourselves have very many questions. Just in hearing the text read aloud, we have no difficulty in understanding that the person who wrote these words thought that something out of order in human life needs to be brought into order. He says this very clearly with the expressions: "reasonable worship of God," "be transformed!" "perfect will of God." Obviously he wants to say that a great truth and a great salvation are here for us, but they are yet concealed and must be brought to light, like the buried treasure in a mine. This means that our life must go through a transformation, and that only through this transformation will that truth and salvation be seen as what they are. It is true, is it not? that we would all like to say yes to that. We would not be here today if we did not more or less recognize that, yes, there is disorder that needs to be given order. Each of us has the secret wish, "Yes, I would like truth and salvation brought to light in my life, in my family!" If we have the distress of our times only a little in our hearts, then we also have within us a presentiment of a hope for that transformation that must occur on earth. Have we not been happy whenever we could think that things will go forward, that a new day will dawn? But we have also sighed whenever we thought, "No, in humanity there is still night, and all remains as it always has been."

The Bible too speaks of this transformation, but the Bible does it in *its own* way. We have to notice above all how *seriously* the Bible talks about it. That is not the agreeable way in which we usually talk about and reflect on life, other people, and ourselves. Our usual way is more like this: "No, it is not so important that the disorder be brought into order; I have so much to do before I concern myself with that, and there are always the unanticipated things that come in between and have to be taken care of. I will still have time later for this transformation, this all-important thing that Paul talks about." But Paul is saying, "No, you have no time to lose; otherwise it could be too late. There really is nothing as important as this, and nothing may come in between."

It must strike us how *radically* Paul speaks. He is not talking about ways to improve things or plans that we might resolve to make, improvements and plans such as those we read about frequently in the newspapers and those we have to deliberate in government and other organizations. In regard to what the Bible is talking about, there is nothing to discuss. When the Bible speaks of transformation, it always means the whole, transformed and made new from the ground up. One might imagine a great plow that tears up the earth, while we usually only scratch the surface with the spades of children. One might even think of those Russian politicians who have tried in the last several months to implement utterly new regulations that would, so to speak, force heaven to come down to earth.[2] But what the Bible intends is far more radical and far more comprehensive than even the boldest human intention. Paul seems to be saying, "Look, you are perishing because you do not go far enough! It would help you, dear brothers and sisters, if you would once be very bold and radical!"

It should further strike us how *personal* Paul's words are. He is not talking past us or over our heads about some beautiful theme for meditation, nor is he speaking in generalities. He is addressing us directly. Now, we are gladly listening observers, and that is the reason why in church one likes to sit at a good distance from the pulpit, as if to say: "I'm only visiting, and I only wish to listen and not really hear." That is why the Bible is not a book for everyone, because it is so direct: it leaves no doubt that it is talking about me! And that is what is meant in Paul's words too. When Paul's words have to do with creating order, the meaning is that *you* must bring this order about. The transformation he is talking about is a transformation in *you*. And truth and salvation come to light because *you* grasp them and bring them to light. In today's text it is impossible not to hear this emphasis on the personal responsibility and work that are laid upon us. And all of what we have said about it— its seriousness and radical nature, and the personal way it comes near to us—makes us again hesitate and waver, even though we would like to say yes. And then awaken in us those questions in which, in all honesty, our no is concealed. And yet we do not want to say no because we feel too clearly *how* good and how necessary it is to say yes.

Let us consider Paul's words that there should be "reasonable worship" among us. Paul's opinion in this is certainly rightly given when we add that all persons really do want to *serve God*. If Paul were to return to life among us today, he would see all the churches and chapels in our cities and villages; he would see Bibles in all the houses. Precisely in our time, he would see in the hearts of so many believers and unbelievers the longing for and the striving toward a higher life and better conditions. He would certainly say to us too, as he spoke once before, "You men of Athens, I see how in every way you fear the gods!" [Acts 17:22, Luther Bible], or as we would render those words today: "how religious and idealistic you are." "Yes, that you are," he would say, "in spite of all your stupidity and unbelief." It is in those who still hold to superstitions; in the many self-righteous persons who have no need to go to church; in the holy zeal of the worldly world reformers, like the Russian Bolsheviks—in all of these there is without any doubt something religious.

And if whatever was needed depended just on that, all would be well and good. The world is full of worship, full of wish and avid striving for something higher and better. If whatever was needed depended just on being religious, 1,900 years ago Paul and the gospel could have left the heathen and Jews in peace, and us with them. But Paul was the kind of person who knew something important about worship: there should be a *reasonable* worship of God. There is an unreasonable way of doing one's work, in which one does a lot, gets tired, but does not accomplish what one was supposed to accomplish. There is an unreasonable eating and drinking, in which one consumes a great deal and is harmed by it rather than nourished. There is an unreasonable reading, in which one consumes whole books, perhaps even half the Bible, and learns nothing; instead, one's thoughts become dissipated and confused. And so there is also an unreasonable worship of God, in which one serves not God, whom one did originally intend to serve, but rather passes God by and finally positions oneself against God.

Paul says that something living, holy, and well pleasing to God belongs to the reasonable worship of God. In the word "living" it is said that our worship of God, in church and at home, on Sunday and during the workweek, must be a searching, working, struggling, a growing and wanting to grow in insightful knowledge and love, just as a living being is supposed to grow. If we want to be like dead stones, with our minds and hearts fully complete and finished, then we will not be able to understand sermons in church, much less the Bible and life itself. Such dead persons, who do not want to search earnestly and sincerely, understand nothing and necessarily pass God by. For God is a living God.

In the word "holy" it is said that in this searching we must intend God and not beautiful thoughts, not what so naturally grows up in our thoughts and rumbles in our hearts. Much avid prayer and sincere striving is for naught because we actually miss God. Ever again when we are pious and have idealistic thoughts, we must detect whether or not we have missed the holy majesty of God, whose thoughts are completely different from ours [cf. Isa. 55:8]. We must ever again see whether we have missed the earnest insight expressed in the words, "Not what I will, but what you will!" [cf. Mark. 14:36 par.]. Then we will be put to shame, and often, although we had meant to do so well.

In the words "well pleasing to God" it is said that our thoughts, words, and works are in need of God's blessing if they are truly to be a worship of God. It is indeed right when we search for God and wish to bring about better conditions in the world, but God must also be able to say yes to the ways and means we have of doing it, for otherwise nothing will come of our efforts. It is indeed good, for example, to pray for and pursue the conversion of persons, but if one cannot put aside an evil way of being that pricks and stings, God is not in it. To give the needy from one's surplus is also good, but whether or not God rejoices in it will depend, for example, on how one has gained the surplus. To turn the world upside down, like the Bolsheviks now want to do, would also be good and much needed, but when they wave around their automatic weapons, the blessing of God cannot be in it. Good, pure persons are needed in order to serve God in a good, pure way, a way that is well pleasing to God. What passes by this good and pure way of being can never lead to the goal.

I think that we now understand a little of what Paul meant when he said that a *sacrifice* is needed for a reasonable worship of God. Here we must look deeply into what is holy. Something must be brought, presented, given. In the words themselves we already notice something of that serious, radical, and personal decision that the Bible requires of us and before which we are rightly perplexed. It is difficult for us and even hurts to give something away, even if it were only a little money that we would rather keep, or a friendly word, when we would rather say something sullen or rude, or an hour of our time that we would rather have for ourselves. The word "sacrifice" always attacks us, like a sharp knife. We would rather serve God in some other way than through sacrifice. In what Paul calls a reasonable worship of God, the giving of a little money is not enough, nor is a good word, nor a little time. One must seriously question whether any of these is a "living sacrifice, holy and well pleasing to God." In fact, they are holy sacrifices only when another and much greater prior sacrifice has taken place, so that it now stands behind them.

For there is only *one* sacrifice that God acknowledges and accepts from us, and if you do not make this sacrifice, the rest collapses like a house of cards. This one sacrifice, according to Paul, consists in "presenting your bodies." What he means is your personhood, your own self, without making a difference between the outer and inner person or of what is spiritual in us and what is natural. He says expressly "your bodies!" and not "your souls!" What Paul means is that there is no difference, that when he speaks of the body he includes the soul. We like to make fine and seemingly intelligent distinctions, as when we say, "Inwardly I am also of this opinion, but outwardly I do not wish to show it"; or, "In my heart I stand on this side too, but with my person I would rather not confess it"; or, "In my soul I want to belong to God, but my body—which means all that I am outwardly in the concealment of my private life, in my family, in my business, in my position in the village—this body of mine may keep going along as usual and often goes fully other ways than the ways of God."

The Bible does not make such fine and clever distinctions. Paul prevents them simply by saying, "Present your bodies as a living sacrifice, holy and well pleasing to God." Here none of those distinctions and the like are acknowledged, such as when one reads worshipfully in the hymnbook on Sunday morning, but on Sunday afternoon goes a completely different way, as many of our teenagers in the confirmation class do. Here one is not allowed to be an idealist that reads good books in the evening, but in the factory during the day acts on the basis of the same principles, or rather lack of principles, as everyone else. Here one is not allowed to be a child of God who today cannot boast enough of the glory of truly trusting God, but tomorrow gets entirely out of sorts when their store of goods has dwindled in some small way.

Such fine distinctions are not possible for Paul. "Present your bodies as a sacrifice!" Then God will receive what God wills to receive from you and what God can use. As long as we do not wish to present our bodies, we wish to give nothing of ourselves. If we have once understood the inner *and* the outer, what belongs to the soul *and* what belongs to the body, one's personal human spirit *and* one's physical person—then we will sacrifice what must be sacrificed; then it will be a living sacrifice, holy and well pleasing to God, just as God is living and holy; then we will give ourselves into the power of God!

That is what is meant by *a reasonable worship of God*. What a pity it is and what a distress that at bottom we all fear the gods so much that we are all so religious and full of endeavor, and yet understand so little of this sacrifice, of giving ourselves, our bodies, as sacrifices into the power of God. Oh, how would the doors that are now closed to us open—all the doors of sin and care before which we so helplessly stand; the doors of persons we do not understand nor they us; the doors of sad social conditions that we presently cannot change—how would truth and salvation come to light, how would the change of things that we wish for happen, if we would only break out of all our so-called worship of God, our religions, convictions, and endeavors! We would break out of all these prisons, over which is written, "My intentions are good," and instead enter into what God intends, into that reasonable worship of God in Spirit and in truth. This is what the Bible places before us in such a great, natural, and healthy way! [cf. John 4:24].

Now we want to take a moment to consider all the questions we have—questions that are really our own answers—when the Bible places us at this point of decision. "Do I understand it? Can I do it? And if I can, how am I to go about it? What will happen to me?" The Bible does not remain silent to these personal sighs, sighs with which we have often left the church on Sunday. It gives us *the* answer that must silence all those questions in which our "No" is concealed. If it were true that this reasonable worship of God is something so foreign and impossible for us, Paul would certainly not have challenged us to do it. But he has yet a little word to say to us, a word that strikes through and cancels out the impossibility. We heard something of it last Sunday: "But now in Christ Jesus you who once were far off have been brought near by the blood of Christ" [Eph. 2:13]. Today he would say it somewhat differently but mean the same thing:

"Dear brothers and sisters, I admonish you *through the mercy of God.* Do you not know that the reasonable worship of God, through which all things become new, has already begun on earth? Do you not know that the sacrifice of the body, which must be presented, has already been presented for all of you? Do you know nothing of the mercy of God, through which a new time for all of you has broken into this world, a time in which human beings no longer must stand outside, hesitant and questioning, swaying back and forth between yes and no? Because now once for all, and for all people, 'Yes' has been said: 'Yes, we want to move out of the prison of our opinions into the opinion of God.' Do you not know that all this is what you have to ask about?"

Dear friend, Paul does not speak from a pulpit or from a lectern, but from the cross of Jesus. It is there, at the cross, where all is put in order that is in disorder in us. That is why Paul can speak so boldly, powerfully, and relentlessly, and yet not ask too much of us. Oh, dear friends, the decision before which we stand is not whether we will or can do it, but only whether we want to see something of the clarity and the power that the mercy of God has revealed precisely at this remarkable place, the cross of Jesus.

Next Sunday we want to begin to wander toward this same place from another side.

COMMENTS

This sermon just doesn't work as a sermon. Barth is far too subtle in his sermon on Romans 12:1–2. He opens with the claim that before the words of Paul we all stand "astonished and full of wonder, and yet rather estranged and disconcerted," but there is little evidence of the preacher's astonishment or wonder in this sermon. While claiming that Paul is talking about "something about which we must decide," something that "would have a huge effect on the way we live," it's difficult to imagine that the humble Safenwilers had a clue as to what on earth the preacher was talking about.

Perhaps obscurity is demanded by the subject matter. Perhaps this is a biblical text that, if honored and respected as God's word, as it is, would be a word that is tough to utter in a cogent, comprehensible sermon. Barth says that Paul is speaking "*seriously*," "*radically*," in a way that is unavoidably "personal." After a swipe at our incurable religiousness (I love that he makes the Russian Bolsheviks the prime example of a world just chock "full of worship"), Barth tackles the significance of "sacrifice." He has a fine excursus on "*presenting your bodies*"—"bodies" signifies that God wants all of us, not just our disembodied "souls." God wants our worldly actions, not merely the exalted, detached thoughts of the "idealist." Then he takes a jab at the parish "confirmation class" (who had so disgraced themselves by their drunkenness at a recent party). But the sermon doesn't do justice to a text that allegedly is "a great plow that tears up the earth," an attack "like a sharp knife."

Barth is thus far too cerebral and abstract in this sermon, interpreting the biblical text as an interesting idea rather than performing the text, doing what the text does within the congregation. He says that Romans 12:1–2 is about "transformation," that this word demands a "radical" decision, that the text "leaves no doubt that it is talking about me!" But then the sermon comes across as arcane, obtuse, and (horror of horrors, for Barth) some sort of disjointed religious address. Surely those who knew firsthand the bogus "sacrifice" of the Great War could be more directly and better engaged with the sacrifice of Christ. It is almost as if the preacher failed to hear his own stunning declaration: "Paul does not speak from a pulpit or from a lectern, but from the cross of Jesus."

When this sermon is compared with Barth's commentary on 12:1–2 in *Romans* (424–38), one is impressed with how much more clear and engaging is the discussion there than here in this sermon on that text. There, Barth says that Romans 12 speaks of "The Great Disturbance," who is the living God. A living, active God who dies on the cross makes our meager human sacrifices and our ethics "dubious," to say the least. Before the great mystery of our atonement, "the voice of the preacher" "is raucous, croaking, and utterly unimpressive" (429). Is this Barth the theologian's justification for Barth the preacher's failure in a sermon on Romans 12:1–2?

If God's grace, as demonstrated in Romans 12:1–2, is "the axe laid to the root of the good conscience," the grand divine rebuke to "modern Lutheranism" with its "weak humanitarianism," then is Pauline radical grace also the negation of engaging, comprehensible, cogent preaching? If grace is that blistering, devastating divine "no" to all human aspirations to divinity, then perhaps grace is also the divine negation of all feeble human attempts to say something coherent about God.

And yet, I still wonder if Barth the preacher could have let Paul the preacher use him to better effect. Paul's words are more coherent than Barth's words about Paul's words. Barth's heavy-handed overlay of his dialectical, crisis theology upon his text tends to smother rather than express the text. He assumes too much for his listeners, is far too subtle in his exposition, and is too abstract in his treatment of a biblical text that bristles with corporeal vividness and stirring exhortation. I find it ironic that a sermon that lifts up the metaphor of the "body" so well fails in structure and embodiment. A sermon without a coherent, discernable body may be a betrayal to an incarnational faith.

Later Barth wrote that our preaching failures help us preachers to

. . . realize how impossible their action is, but that they may still look beyond its uncertainty and focus on the fact of revelation. This will give them confidence that the revealed word of God which is at work in their action will cover their weakness and corruptness, and that they are promised a righteousness which they themselves can never give to what they do. Knowing the forgiveness of sins, they may do their work in simple obedience, no longer, then, as a venture, but in the belief that God has commanded it.[3]

Our preaching failures drive us into the arms of a forgiving, merciful God, force us to cling to the "fact of revelation," to preach a biblical text not because it works, or gives us or the congregation joy in the preaching, but rather because "God has commanded it."

It's quite a challenge to be a truly biblical preacher. One must not only say what the text says, but one must also say it as the text says. The artistic form of the biblical text, the rhetoric employed, the dynamic of the text—these are not incidental or extraneous to the message of the text. We not only preach what the Bible preaches, but we preachers are also invigorated, and our listeners are engaged, by how the Bible preaches. We preachers ought to be at least as attentive to form and design as the biblical writers themselves. Theology without wings is not yet a sermon, no matter how good the theology.

I smile at Barth's ending: "Next Sunday we want to begin to wander toward this same place from another side." Now who in the congregation could resist such enticement to return next Sunday!

May 19, 1918

Acts 2:1–4

When the day of Pentecost had come, they were all together in one place. And suddenly from heaven there came a sound like the rush of a violent wind, and it filled the entire house where they were sitting. Divided tongues, as of fire, appeared among them, and a tongue rested on each of them. All of them were filled with the Holy Spirit and began to speak in other languages, as the Spirit gave them ability.

Dear friends!

God is not far from any one of us; for "in him we live and move and have our being" [Acts 17:27–28]. God is the God of all people, of the Jews and the heathen, of believers and unbelievers. The Father in heaven "makes his sun rise on the evil and on the good, and sends rain on the righteous and on the unrighteous" [Matt. 5:45]. "Where can I go from your spirit? Or where can I flee from your presence? If I ascend to heaven, you are there; if I make my bed in Sheol, you are there. If I take the wings of the morning and settle at the farthest limits of the sea, even there your hand shall lead me, and your right hand shall hold me fast" [Ps. 139:7–10]. In spite of all the differences and oppositions in the way we humans relate to God, we cannot think broadly enough, not boldly enough, not great enough of the way God relates to us. What significance do the differences of our belief have before God? "For God has imprisoned all in disobedience so that he may be merciful to all" [Rom. 11:32]. In all human souls there stands written in the same inviolable, incomparable way: "Lord, you have created us for you, and our heart is restless until it rests in you" [Augustine]. Human beings belong to God, just as nature belongs to God. It is true, is it not? that we understand much better that all lives and moves in God when we think of nature. In nature there are far fewer disturbances and confusions than in the lives of human beings, although they are not lacking there either. Nature is closer to its origin than we are, and in

57

nature the most inner being of things comes to appearance with greater vigor and clarity. This inner being is an eternal life, a creative wisdom, a fullness of imperishable beauty and power. This has been demonstrated in these last several spring days to every really open and unhurried view into the rich realm of nature's life.

But *human beings too* belong to God. There is something in us all that comes more from God and strives more to return to God than all that speaks to us in nature. Human beings are created to be God's eye, ear, and, yes, God's heart in the midst of created life. Human beings are created to think God's thoughts and to do God's works. We cannot separate ourselves from this determination of our being. It is true, is it not? that we only have to be told of this in a clear and gracious way, and we do again remember that we have a home in God. We certainly are sinners, but even our most problematic entanglements and confusions are actually only a shaking and pulling on the ties that bind us to God. We are dull and indifferent, but not really toward God as God truly is, but because God has become so strange and incomprehensible. We are unbelievers, but our protest against faith is actually far more a cry against something false that has come between God and us than a real separation from God.

All the errors and lies of humanity are only hardened, perverted, and sick [versions of] truths that have their origin in God. There would be no evil if there were no good. The fury with which nations today plunge into war, the greed with which we serve Mammon, the severity with which you defend your rights, the lack of truthfulness with which you conceal yourself from yourself and others, the bitterness with which you close yourself in and others out—all of these we have from God. For they are all forms of powers, goods, and lordship stolen from God and spoiled by our evil being. But there is always something in our evil being that wants to return to God, something that wants to clean and purify itself of all the spoilage. We are indeed right when we say, "We did not mean it in such a bad way," for the evil, satanic things that ever again appear in us really do not belong to our innermost being. Rather, our innermost being is of God and awaits salvation, like the soft, sweet kernel of spring wants to burst its hard shell.

How do I know this? From where do I take the competence and the courage to say it, when all of life—your life, my life, and that of all humanity—seems clearly to witness against it? But I am not dreaming or fooling myself, nor am I basing what I say on thoughts of my own—my own thoughts would naturally go in a different direction. I am rather only saying what today *must* be said, if we are to speak of the relationship between God and human beings. What has happened in Christ is what forces us to say that human beings belong to God! Without Christ one could laughingly deride such talk as deception, dreaming, and imagination. Without Christ it would be at best no more than a nice idea. But through Christ it has become the most certain of all certainties that we human beings can know. Through Christ *the whole earth*, all creatures and all humanity, stands in the light of heaven.

It may well be that we no longer see Christ as we should, as the one in whom God loves the world [cf. John 3:16], but we do see the light that beams from him into the world. For we can do no other than understand our life in this light. It is no accident and no mere invention when we know, clearly proclaim, and so gladly hear it said that evil is not our nature, but an abnormality, a perversion of our nature. And the divine is truthfully not the most distant thing from us, but the nearest thing to us. What is good is not foreign to us but what is most our own deeply within us. Our most inner being is a will and a wish to love and be loved. It can indeed be covered over and buried, but its life can never be extinguished. In our soul slumbers a whole new world of goodness and joy, and it very much wants to break powerfully forth today. All this *is* real, as we have said, and we can neither deny it nor keep silent about it because the beams of light that go out from Christ are also in us!

We certainly see that *other thing* that would call all this wrong and false. We see that we stand under the accusation of not being true to God, that in small as well as large and very important matters we give God not honor but dishonor. We see the shadow that falls from this accusation on our whole life. We see how weak, broken, and uncertain we are and our thinking and speech are, because we have a bad conscience. We also see the powers of sin that are loosened against us through our not being true to God. We see that we often, even with the best intentions, hardly know what direction to take in order to avoid falling from one foolish mistake into another. We see the penalty of nothingness and the perishing character of all our being and doing that results from our unfaithfulness.

We must take all of this seriously, but it is no longer *the only thing* we can take seriously, for through Christ the unfaithfulness of not being true to God does not have to be. We see the abyss that separates us from the truth and glory of God, but today we also see the way that leads over the abyss. We see the host of our enemies, who keep us from the life we should live, but we also see that these enemies are only fighting a rearguard action, that they are retreating, because their main force has been defeated. We see the walls of the prison or hospital or our personal shell, or whatever the circumstances in which we find ourselves might be, but we also see through an open window into a different situation, where God's faithfulness triumphs over our unfaithfulness. For there humanity has found itself; there the accusation, whose shadow lies upon us, is extinguished; there is forgiveness of sins; there the powers of darkness that now hold us captive are themselves taken captive [cf. Eph. 4:8], for they have found their master. There God "will wipe every tear from their eyes. Death will be no more; mourning and crying and pain will be no more, for the first things have passed away" [Rev. 21:4].

Today we see into this different situation, and we can no longer act as if we had *not* seen it. Christ has not lived, died, and been resurrected in vain. In heaven and on earth something has changed in our favor, and we now have new ground beneath our feet. Today, when we consider our life and our world, we can no longer think and act on the basis of sin and death, or of war, or of today's circumstances and situations generally, or of the imperfection and evil of human nature, or of the weakness and mortality of our existence. As true as all these are, there is no longer any benefit in taking them more seriously than they deserve. Today we have to think and act on the basis of God's lordship and dominion, which is over all things and peoples.

For in Christ the secret of our lives has been revealed, namely, that God *is*: God *is* the conqueror of death, *is* the world's origin and goal, *is* the end of all horror and wrongheadedness, *is* the God who forgives and covers our sin, *is* the God who is stronger than all our unfaithfulness. If God is, then humanity belongs to God. No longer can we fail to recognize this. It is the one perception that exactly today, at Pentecost, comes to light in a myriad of ways. At Pentecost the disciples of Jesus were of one mind and heart in this perception. And this deepest of all perceptions has led us to be together here today.

And yet it is true, is it not? that *something is missing*. If we are completely honest, we have to say that something essential is missing. We have the feeling that this essential thing was also missing for the disciples of Jesus *before* Pentecost. Consider nature once more: We observe the play of a colorful butterfly; we sink ourselves into the wonderful structure of a flower; our eyes become lost in the mysterious expanse of the stars. Even with the bright and friendly light that shines upon us in Christ, we cannot avoid the impression that the world of nature has a more immediate and more real relationship to God than our human world. In all of nature there is such a remarkable breath and scent of divine reality. We rejoice over the truth that we have in Christ, but it is true, is it not? that we often ask ourselves whether there is a reality in Christ and a life with God like that of the flowers or the buzzing bees, a life truly in the strength and harmony of the God to whom we belong and from whose hand no one can snatch us away [cf. John 10:28].

We want not only to know that we are in God's hand, but also to be what we should be as persons who are truly in God's hand. We want in a more real sense to be true to God and free of sin and to overcome sorrow, both our own and that of others. We want to burst the bonds of Mammon, establish peace, and cast aside the powers of death. We want not just to know about God's blessing but also to have and possess God's blessing. We want not simply to look into the true situation of our life revealed by Christ but also to be placed into it. We want not only to have new ground beneath our feet but also to walk on this ground. We want not only to carry the light of Christ within us but also to have our thinking and doing illumined by that light.

We rejoice to hear that we belong to God—we cannot hear it enough—yet we want not just to hear it, but also really to belong to God. In us all there is a hunger for this wealth of life in God and this being in God, for being immersed in the stream of the life of God that heaven and earth proclaim.

We have on occasion gone home from *church* full of the happy certainty that, yes, God *is*, and beside God there are no other gods [Isa. 45:5]. But hardly were we at home than this hunger for life and being in God came over us more than ever, perhaps so strongly that we almost wished not to have heard about it at all—not if we were only to hear about it and nothing more. Oh, this church, with its eternal talking and hearing about God, yet in which our last and deepest longing remains unfulfilled!

We have read the *Bible*, and all, all seemed to become clear: how the world is so beautiful and simple if we only understand it from the right point of view—which is no longer impossible, since in Christ our eyes have been opened. But when the Bible opened ever so many windows to Jerusalem, it was still only a looking toward the holy city and not going in, not entrance into it. We saw a greeting and waving to us from afar, but we did not have the presence of the divine in our thinking and doing. Oh, this Bible, how it shows us this divinity so clearly and yet abandons us when it is a matter of our taking and having it ourselves.

We have *prayed* and found God, and yet really *not* found God, for what we have found was at best a new *knowledge* of God. Certainly we have thought new, great, bold, and free thoughts, and made new, great, bold, and free decisions, such as are emerging everywhere in humanity in our time. For again, Christ has not been awakened from the dead in vain. Entire nations have experienced a rush of such new thoughts about life, as from mighty storm winds—for example, Russia in the last several years. But how painful it is when we ever again have to recognize that, for all the plans we make, we cannot really build; that with all our new ideas there are indeed contractions, but no actual birth of new being. Yes, how remarkable and how painful that there always remains *such a great step* from divine truth to the reality of this truth, from the light in Christ, which we have, to the power of Christ that we would so much like to have.

But God cannot mean that in Christ we should be redeemed and yet not redeemed, liberated and yet not liberated, blessed and yet not blessed. We also do not mean this in the church when we talk and hear of God, when we baptize and celebrate the Lord's Supper. We never mean that all this should be simply talking and hearing and beckoning. If we did not intuitively seek something greater, better, more real, we would have long since given it all up; no one would want to listen to us, and there would be no pastors. Obviously the Bible does not mean that either, for with all the windows that it opens for us, with all the great and true things it shows us, it seems also to whisper: "Yes, dear friend, here you have all you need to know and can know. I have told you and I say it ever again: God is, and you belong to God, if . . ." This mysterious "if" remains.

It is an "if" about which the Bible only seldom expressly speaks, and yet the Bible speaks about it on every page. We sense it very clearly when we pray. Oh, we need not pray in vain; we need never forget what is necessary when we pray; we can find what we seek. But there is an "if" that—assuming its condition is met—makes our prayer real prayer, just as it makes God's Word the real Word of God. We strongly sense this "if" standing above all thoughts and decisions that ripen in us; we do so all the more when they are of a higher order, when they have to do with thoughts and decisions about the meaning of our life. Above the inner struggles and afflictions of the restless and hopeful time in which we live, this "if" very prominently stands out. It is the condition and the cause that determines whether something really new will be born, as in the time of the Reformation and as in all times of the Spirit; or whether, in spite of all the restlessness and longing for something new, in spite of all that we know in Christ, nothing new will be born.

We can now understand what happened to the disciples of Jesus at Pentecost. You will note that I have just said the word "Spirit." The Spirit is the fulfillment of the promise, the presence of the divine, the reality of Christ. The Spirit is the step from recognizing to being, from knowing to having. The Spirit fulfills the condition of the "if," so that it is canceled out, and puts in its place the words "It is!" The disciples of Jesus had no need to envy the divine reality in the existence of the butterfly and the stars, for they themselves stood in the midst of that reality. Where they were, the forgiveness of sins was not merely proclaimed but actually given; not only was sorrow calmed with much comforting, but the sick also were made healthy. There was not only talk about God and hearing about God, but God also stood behind every word that was spoken and heard, making it clear that it was God's word, living and powerful, filled with seriousness, joy, and clarity, so that it was spoken and heard as it was intended, so that it fell as fruitful seed on fertile soil. Not only did they know about the great change in our favor that had taken place on earth and in heaven, but they also knew the power that had brought about this change, that had descended from heaven and was in the disciples, driving them to witness. Not only had Christ died and risen, but his death in obedience and his resurrection in righteousness came to them as a reality and became their own, so that Paul could later write, "I live, and yet not I, but Christ in me!" [Gal. 2:20, Luther's Bibel], and on another occasion: "So we are now ambassadors for Christ" [2 Cor. 5:20, Luther's Bibel].—That is what we do not have. That is what has not yet happened to us, in spite of the churches and the separatist chapels, in spite of all the Bible reading and prayer, in spite of all the good thoughts that may be stirring in us today.

It is a good thing that the biblical story of Pentecost is told as a genuine *miracle story*. In it we should recognize that a definite and extraordinary act of God is needed if we are to move from "if" to "It is!" A sound like the rush of a violent wind vertically from above, tongues of fire that rested on each of them, the gift of speaking in foreign tongues—all this makes it clear that there is nothing ordinary or self-evident in the act of the Spirit being poured out onto human beings. It is not something in our control, but something we can only receive. For all too long we have not understood that this act of God is precisely what is decisive, essential, and most important in human being's relationship to God. And because we have not understood this, it has been lost to us.

For all too long we have thought that the Spirit is *self-evidently* present, while, on the contrary, the truth is that the outpouring of the Spirit should have continued as the miraculous act of God. Because of this misunderstanding, the Spirit has not moved as it wants to move, but has had to stand still, with the result that the Spirit can be found almost only in the Bible and in a few spiritual times in subsequent history. In a small way, in little "drops," so to speak, the Spirit has also appeared here and there in our time and in our lives, as a sign of what must occur, and yet does not occur. For all too long we have confused the Holy Spirit with *our human spirit*. That is why our human spirit, which knows the truth so well, now hungers for the reality of the truth. For all too long we have found our consolation only in the mere *knowledge* of God; we today have perhaps more of this knowledge than the apostles themselves. For all too long we have neglected asking about God as God truly is; we have neglected to appeal to God and to call on God for what only God can do. That is why we are poor in all our wealth, why we find ourselves in the remarkable circumstance of knowing so much that is true about God and yet not true at all, because God has not yet made it true within us. And this is because we have been rather too comfortable with things as they are.

But if we are no longer comfortable, if we are not finished and done, so that we accept things as they are, then neither is God finished and done. In heaven and on earth something presses, urges toward a continuation of God's miraculous acts. "The time is surely coming, says the Lord GOD, when I will send a famine on the land; not a famine of bread, or a thirst for water, but of hearing the words of the LORD. They shall wander from sea to sea, and from north to east; they shall run to and fro, seeking the word of the LORD, but they shall not find it" [Amos 8:11–12]. "Then afterward I will pour out my spirit on all flesh!" [Joel 2:28].

Amen.

COMMENTS

Barth, who in *Romans* became known as the theologian who stressed the great distance of God from humanity, here preaches a Pentecost sermon that asserts, "We cannot think broadly enough, not boldly enough, not great enough of the way God relates to us." God is near to us. God is relational. And yet that claim *"God is not far"* requires nuance.

When Barth asks rhetorically, "How do I know this?" one might expect him to say "because the Bible tells me," or since this is Pentecost, "because the Holy Spirit has revealed it to me." But he mentions only Christ as source of his knowledge of God's nearness. Even Scripture is mute without Christ. Of the Bible, Barth says, "When the Bible opened ever so many windows to Jerusalem, it was still only a looking toward the holy city and not going in, not entrance into it. We saw a greeting and waving to us from afar, but we did not have the presence of the divine in our thinking and doing. Oh, this Bible, how it shows us this divinity so clearly and yet abandons us when it is a matter of our taking and having it ourselves." With sentiments on biblical inspiration like that, it is odd that anyone ever accused Barth of "biblicism," but they did.

Later Barth would be charged with "Christomonism" in his insistence that everything we think about the Christian faith must flow from and return to Christ. We are in a sad state, in our sin and despair, yet because God has come near to us in Christ, we know that our distance from God is not the final word about our situation.

A "shadow" falls over all human life, in even its most bright and appealing aspects. We look at nature and feel that the honeybee is closer than humanity to the Creator. The bleak situation of humanity is a fact that must be taken with complete "seriousness." And yet, there is another fact, a countertestimony about the human being that must be taken with even more seriousness. When Barth stresses some point or unpacks some theological concept, he does not do so with sermon illustrations nor does he engage in any sort of explanation. Rather, he utilizes metaphor, paradox, dialectical images. So now the preacher displays a dazzling array of metaphors to engage the congregation:

> We see the abyss that separates us from the truth and glory of God, but today we also see the way that leads over the abyss. We see the host of our enemies, who keep us from the life we should live, but we also see that these enemies are only fighting a rearguard action, that they are retreating, because their main force has been defeated. We see the walls of the prison or hospital or our personal shell, . . . but we also see through an open window into a different situation, where God's faithfulness triumphs over our unfaithfulness. . . . The accusation, whose shadow lies upon us, is extinguished; . . . the powers of darkness that now hold us captive are themselves taken captive [cf. Eph. 4:8], for they have found their master.

All this evidence for the nearness of God is "the one perception that exactly today, at Pentecost, comes to light in a myriad of ways." This seems to me a fair reading of Acts 2. The Holy Spirit descends— God has come near. And yet it is noteworthy that this divine proximity doesn't have much content in this sermon. In Acts 2, people speak, people hear, specific Scriptures are called forth in validation of the event. Pentecost ends with Peter, inflamed by the Holy Spirit, preaching to a scoffing mob and converting many. Yet Barth mentions none of that. Furthermore, Pentecost is often presented as the birth of the church, the pneumatic foundation of a new community where old divisions of language have been healed and a new age begins. Not a word from the preacher about that. The preacher who so frequently uses polemic against the church would be loath to interpret Acts 2 as ecclesiology. Rather, the descent of the Spirit is interpreted as a matter of "perception," a solution to the general human dilemma more than the birth of a peculiar new spiritual community.

Then the sermon makes a rather surprising turn, considering what we have seen of Barth's previous sermons. In spite of the preacher's reservations about our innate human ability to connect with God, his disparagement of the church and "religion" as vehicles of revelation and redemption, even his misgivings about the Bible's ability to speak to us—in spite of all this, the preacher says, "God cannot mean that in Christ we should be redeemed and yet not redeemed, liberated and yet not liberated, blessed and yet not blessed." Now the preacher moves from reservations, warnings, and questions to a strong, positive declaration that God's nearness is not a dim possibility; it is a present reality.

Schleiermacher believed that human beings can have immediate perception, utterly unhindered, of God, directly, intuitively. Barth was convinced that there is no truly Christian theology that is not exclusively mediated by Jesus Christ. This conviction seemed to grow ever more vivid in his early years as a pastor. So how, in this sermon, is God a present reality? How is it possible that redemption, proclaimed and described in Scripture, becomes a fact for us? "We can now understand what happened to the disciples of Jesus at Pentecost. You will note that I have just said the word 'Spirit.' The Spirit is the fulfillment of the promise, the presence of the divine, the reality of Christ." The preacher has thus saved the best for last. He has spent most of his sermon casting us in that dilemma to which only the Holy Spirit can minister. "The Spirit is the step from recognizing to being, from knowing to having."

God is near only as God, not as the result of any human contribution. The Holy Spirit has little in common with the "human spirit." Thus Barth praises Acts 2 for being "a genuine *miracle story*. In it we should recognize that a definite and extraordinary act of God is needed if we are to move from 'if' to 'It is!' A sound like the rush of a violent wind vertically from above. . . ." In the account of Pentecost, even the spiritually stupid among us can clearly see that this is a miracle, an act of God, a gift from on high. Here is undeniably God, "the Spirit being poured out onto human beings. It is not something in our control, but something we can only receive." It is as he writes in *Romans*: The grace of God is "pure, absolute, vertical miracle" (60).

The preacher concludes with comforting speculation that this message is most accessible to those who are not too comfortable with "things as they are." In *Romans*, Barth notes how the coming of Christ overturns our usual intellectual distinctions: "God pronounces those who are awake to be asleep, believers to be unbelievers, the righteous to be unrighteous" (70). The descent of the Spirit promises that those who do not know shall know. Those who do not have shall have—which is a nice word to hear from one who has just preached such a thick, packed, theologically jammed sermon.

I love the last paragraph of the sermon. First there are devastating words from Amos about the coming "famine" of the word, where frustrated seekers of God run to and fro trying to get a word from the Lord only to receive dead silence. Then Joel's effusive promise, surely delivered with a shout: God's Spirit, God's Word, God's presence poured out on all! All.

John 1:1–5

In the beginning was the Word, and the Word was with God, and the Word was God. He was in the beginning with God. All things came into being through him, and without him not one thing came into being. What has come into being in him was life, and the life was the light of all people. The light shines in the darkness, and the darkness did not comprehend it. (alt.)[1]

1. "*The life was the light of all people. The light shines* in the darkness. . . ." We live from this truth. This shining light is *like the air* we breathe: we live from it without thinking about it. All that we know and have that is joyful, beautiful, and beloved comes from this shining light. But, like children who reject their parents, we can be ungrateful and forget the source from which we receive the best we have. Yet the source never ceases to flow, and we never cease to drink from it. We can indeed sit in a corner with the minuscule light of our own wisdom and righteousness, and act as if this little light were the only right one in the world, the one that should illumine God and all other human beings. Even such minuscule lights would have no brightness at all, if it were not for that great shining light; without knowing it, we have kindled our little lights from that light. It is impossible to hide from that shining light behind the curtains of our excuses and misunderstandings, behind the bushes of our sins and lies, like Adam and Eve [cf. Gen. 3:8]. It shines, if only a little, through all of that. Even the deepest recesses into which we may creep are not entirely dark, and we are glad of it, in spite of all our contradictions and lack of understanding. This shining light is given, and we live from it.

The light shines. We may hear this as a message of *joy,* good news, gospel for us and the whole world. We may proclaim it courageously and *defiantly* against all the darkness of our time; against the darkness in our own hearts, in our community, in the hospitals, mental institutions, and prisons; against the darkness in our conversations with one another and in the newspapers that we read; against the darkness that darkens so many sickbeds and the beds of the dying; and against the pernicious darkness of our social conditions.[2] Without hesitation we may proclaim *against all darkness:* the light shines. It remains true to itself; it remains what it is even in the deepest darkness, and that is why it shines. Because it is true, we may be courageous and defiant. There is no reason to *doubt* and despair, to give up, to think only somber and hopeless thoughts about ourselves, our community, and today's world. There is no reason *to draw back* from any power of darkness. If we could forget what is essential and most important, there would be cause to draw back; but we can never entirely forget it. The light shines. That is what must be and remain most important, over against all that is otherwise true, all that otherwise occupies and fills our minds and hearts and causes us to be burdened with care.

For *in the Savior,* whose birth we will celebrate at Christmas, the light is a power of God for all who are honest and upright. *Based only on ourselves,* we human beings *really do not understand life.* Based on ourselves, on what we think, decide, and do, we will always be in error in answering the most important questions, even with the best of intentions. We see *so many* people whose intentions are good and mean well, but who are in the greatest error about life and whose actions are very dark, only because they base everything they do on themselves. In the previous sermon we spoke of the closed *doors* that confront a person who willingly lives and understands life based on oneself alone. We live in a world full of confusion and lack of understanding, full of violence and distress, and all of it comes from this: willing to live *based on ourselves.* Now, however, in the Savior something beyond us, something *from the other side,* has begun to move. The *life* has now revealed itself. The *truth* has appeared. The *eternal* has come into time. The *love of God* has been poured out [cf. Rom. 5:5]. *God* has given the course of the world another direction.

It is as if God had said to humanity, "Now things are based not on you, but on me! Based on you, on your thought and actions, there was *sin;* based on me, there is forgiveness and the power of a new life. Based on you, there is *distress and affliction;* based on me, there is help and salvation. Based on you, there is always *opposition, one against the other;* based on me, there is togetherness and being for one another. Based on you, there are all kinds of *false valuations* of greatness, position, money, education; based on me, there is humility and fellowship. Based on you, there is coarseness, violence, severity, and much noisemaking; based on me, there is what is fine, quiet, interior. Based on you, the most exalted lord and ruler is death; based on me, there is eternal life."

That is how we might imagine God telling us of *the change that has come about* through Jesus Christ, a fact that can never be undone. In the Savior an *understanding*, a perceiving recognition of true life, has come into humanity. As long as we are based on ourselves, this true life remains a mystery, something concealed and locked away; but it has now been opened to humanity and is its light. The honest and upright recognize the change, and for them the light shines clearly, the light that has risen over the old world and brings the announcement of a new world. For the honest and upright the life that has appeared in Jesus Christ has not appeared in vain.

One could certainly ask whether it is really true that the Savior has kindled such a light in the world, whether we are not in complete darkness in spite of the Savior. Are there honest and upright people at all? That is precisely the question that Advent asks *us*! *We* should not look around and ask, "Are there any honest and upright people?" as if such persons should come down from heaven; it is enough that the truth has come to us from heaven in Jesus Christ.

It is God who asks *us,* "Can what I have spoken become true among you? *Where* are the honest and upright people who willingly hear and understand what I have said? Where are the bright, open eyes that can see and understand the light? Who truly hears and obeys the joyful message that the light shines? Please understand that *for me* all is in good order: the light shines, the truth is made known to you, and the knowledge necessary for salvation is in you. But is all in good order *for you? Can the light now* defy the darkness? Can it triumph? Do you who are Christians, 'Christ-persons,' do you see something of the change in all things, of the revelation of the life that is in this name you bear? Are you what you say you are? *And your world?* Your poor, your sick, your weak, your sinners and godless people, your mockers and slanderers: do they in any way sense or recognize that Christ the Savior has come? Does a breath of comfort, healing, and wellness go out into the sick world from you who are Christians? Have you done your part to let the light that you have *penetrate* into your families, into your social circumstances, into the relations of different peoples and nations to one another? I have *laid hold of* you, but have you understood me? In pure goodness I have *found* you and drawn you to me [cf. Jer. 31:3 KJV]—but do you seek me? I have given you righteousness out of my grace—but are you now righteous?"

Suddenly the tables are turned; now we are the ones being asked. The question that we want to ask of God is *turned* back on us. We are asked whether the light of Christmas really is light. So the answer that God gives our questions is his calling us to account, his asking us what we have made of the light that has long since been given us at Christmas. And now it is up to us to give answer to God.

2. What are we to say? The text says, "*The light shines in the darkness, and the darkness did not comprehend it.*" Over against the obvious, clear fact of the light, there is the other enigmatic, confused, incomprehensible fact of the *darkness*. Certainly *we live* from the light, but how does it happen that we can live as if without it? How does it happen that we live with so many things on the basis of which one *cannot live:* wrong pride, wrong fear, wrong love, wrong hate, wrong reverence, and wrong contempt? How does it happen that we want to put so much value on what is worthless and to depend on what is in decay? How does it happen that we so easily exchange God for a thousand greater and smaller *idols?* And how does it happen that as a consequence our life is *not real life* but only passing the time in dull, unhappy, and restless living?

Yes, certainly, *the light shines.* But how does it happen that we so *seldom risk relying on this fact,* standing on it and making it valid in our thoughts, words, and acts? Why do we have so *little courage* and so little humility? Why do dark things so quickly frighten us, and why are we so remarkably quick to forget that we were frightened? Why are we *almost always* to be found where one fearfully bows before the power of evil? When it really matters, why do we seek and find so many self-righteously clever *reasons* to place ourselves on the side of darkness? Why are *nonessential things always so important,* and the essential thing so unimportant? And how does it happen that we are constantly more in the darkness than in the light, more in concealment than in open clarity, more anxious than brave, more in judgment than in grace? How does that happen?

Yes, certainly, the Savior is our light—but is it not odd that we *allow* so little of the light of the Savior *to enter into* our work, into our relations to other persons and to the events of our time, into conversations in our families, into our dealings with the civil authorities and the organizations to which we belong? Why do we always take *everything so seriously* and find everything to be so important, except for what has become serious and important through Christ? Why do we constantly so smartly and practically deliberate all possible matters, except for those that are necessary in view of the change in all things that has happened through the Savior? Is it any wonder when under these circumstances the light of Christmas, the redemption of the world, the coming of the kingdom of God becomes uncertain and *doubtful*? Is it any wonder when they become something one hears about in church with only half an ear, something that one not for a moment risks including in one's actions outside the church, because one must constantly fear that it is not true? Is it any wonder, when it often seems that the appearance of the life in Christ was *for nothing*, that it is *not* the light of human beings?

Dear friends! We must understand this situation as it is. When we ask where the light of the world is to be found, we can give God and ourselves only one answer: Here is the darkness, and the darkness has not comprehended the light. We *cannot explain* the darkness or give reasons for it. It is inexplicable, unfathomable, without meaning or foundation. It is what should have long since disappeared, and yet it is still here. It is the impossible, and yet this impossibility *is possible*! What cannot at all be *is*! What is absolutely wrong and senseless stands there like a large block, boasting, as it were, of its presence. "The darkness does not comprehend the light." The darkness is *not a ghost,* not fate, not a law of nature. It has a will, an evil will. It can comprehend, and it cannot comprehend. It exists as personal being. All of this is an indication that the darkness is not something simply in the air; it is not in heaven or beneath the earth. It is rather in human beings.

Only the human being is capable of such artful, refined deceit, the very opposite of what is honest and upright. Only through this dishonesty and lack of uprightness does the human being, who comprehends the light, at the same time will *not to comprehend* it. The human being wills not to understand what one understands. The human being *defies* what one so sincerely wants, *closing self* to what is most necessary and simple. Based on human beings, *life in the world* becomes dark when it could have long since become light. The whole enigma of the darkness is *in us ourselves*. We are *in contradiction* with ourselves: we *have* the truth and we *reject* the truth, and in the same moment we reject it, we *thirst* for it. We are not honest and upright.

3. There are a few things to say about this contradiction. The fact that we are *not honest and upright* must burn painfully. It must be painful that the contradiction and all these questions are indelibly present. It must be painful that the world is dark because of *the darkness in us*. This condition is *not tolerable*. It should be completely clear to us that

there can be no peace as long as this condition persists: no peace in the soul, nor in our social and economic relations, nor among the different peoples and nations, nor anywhere in heaven or earth. As long as the contradiction is not resolved, what is most important is left undone. Once we have only minimally recognized how things really are, we may *no longer* sleep. We are still much too mediocre, much too cunning, much too cautious. In this condition we will make no progress. "Now is the moment for you to wake from sleep" [Rom. 13:11]. What is needed are persons who willingly and *personally take on* this serious need, cry out for change, and work for it. There can be no standstill in the relationship of light and darkness; the war must go on.

The message of Advent about the coming light requires that we become people of Advent, people who persistently await the victorious light. Where there are such people, Christmas can happen. Christ waits for people who will not compromise the light with darkness, neither in themselves nor in anything else, but who are moved by the serious need for the light of Christ and who are aware of whence the help comes. May God give that we may go forth to the festival of Christmas as moved and motivated people. Then we will experience Christmas with the gifts of grace and blessing.

COMMENTS

"*The life was the light of all people. The light shines* in the darkness." Barth opens this 1918 Advent sermon with joyous, unrestrained, triumphant affirmation. The preacher who seems so impressed with the elusiveness of the living God and the arcane quality of biblical truth now celebrates undeniable, unfettered revelation. Possibility and potentiality have now become fulfilled. The light shines.

The light shines so brightly that "it is impossible to hide from that shining light behind the curtains of our excuses." Against all odds, all objections and reservations, "the light shines." This is no fragile, twinkling light. The preacher takes a surprisingly defiant tone:

We may proclaim it courageously and *defiantly* against all the darkness of our time; against the darkness in our own hearts, in our community, in the hospitals, mental institutions, and prisons; against the darkness in our conversations with one another and in the newspapers that we read; against the darkness that darkens so many sickbeds and the beds of the dying; and against the pernicious darkness of our social conditions. Without hesitation we may proclaim *against all darkness:* the light shines.

Later some critics charged that Barth did not really take seriously the possibility of disbelief. He was so exuberantly confident in the triumph and the irresistibility of the revelation of God in Jesus Christ that doubt and disbelief became a kind of impossibility. More than one commentator accused Barth of "universalism," in which he appeared to have a higher regard for those outside church, as recipients of Christ's virtually irresistible salvation, than for those inside church who seemed to think that the scope of Christ's triumph was limited to them. At one point Bonhoeffer wondered if Barth was guilty of a "positivism of revelation," and Tillich complained that Barth ignored the possibility of doubt with his take-it-or-leave-it theology. Many years later, at a lecture at the University of Chicago, when one of the respondents observed that many in the lecture hall were not Christians, Barth responded that that was of absolutely no consequence to him. What believers and unbelievers know or don't know about the fact that in Jesus Christ, God was reconciling the world—that is of no fundamental concern to Barth.

Judging from these sermons, one can say that Barth appears resolutely untroubled by modern doubt and skepticism. He is confident that it is of the nature of the Trinity to speak, to reveal, and to disclose, and that the modern world's intellectual reservations are not to be taken too seriously. For the preacher to attempt apologetics, argument, and persuasion is to risk compromising gospel truth, trimming our message to the alleged limits of the narrow modern mind, and thus casting doubt upon the power of God to speak. It is the preacher's business to proclaim the truth, not to worry over human qualms and misgivings. "The light shines. That is what must be and remain most important, over against all that is otherwise true." The light shines!

This sermon was preached in the year that the Great War had ended. Barth had also at last completed *Romans*. Perhaps that note of fruition and culmination contributes to the sermon's opening joy. Yet 1918 was also a time of the general strike in Switzerland, great financial crisis, industrial unrest, and class conflict. This year Oswald Spengler published *The Decline of the West*, signaling the beginning of a time of European pessimism and uncertainty. Thus this sermon embodies in its opening both the joyous theme of "light!" and a somber admission of humanity's collective love of "darkness."

We live in this odd contradiction whereby the light shines, yet we refuse to be honest about the light. The mess we're in is due exclusively to our irrational determination to live on the basis of our own pitiful lights rather than come to the Light. The gloomy modern world is the result of our being "willing to live *based on ourselves.*" We stupidly stumble in the darkness rather than walk in the light. Still, "*life* has now revealed itself. The *truth* has appeared. The *eternal* has come into time. The *love of God* has been poured out," and all our stupid, darkened stumbling cannot quench the light.

At this point it seems to me that Barth misses some great opportunities to be specific, to allow the sermon to touch down in concrete, current realities. Words like "life," "truth," and "eternal" cause the sermon to begin to float upward, wafting out over the congregation and touching down nowhere. I find myself, in Barth's early sermons, longing for this high-sounding theology to alight somewhere. An all-too-intellectualized gospel is preached in most of these sermons. My desire is justified, I think, particularly in this sermon that aspires to be based upon the Fourth Gospel, where "the Word became flesh and lived among us" (1:14).

I expect that Barth's preaching is so determined by his rebellion against a theology based upon human experience, so convinced that nothing is happening in current events, in political machinations, in the hearts and minds of the preacher or the congregation—nothing that can match what is going on in the Bible. Barth never argues in his sermons; he asserts. Thus we have heard in these sermons hardly any illustration, reference to contemporary concerns, or citation of external authorities. None of that is of great help in reading Scripture, Barth seems to say. None of that gives us anywhere to stand or a key to insightful interpretation. We stand before God empty-handed. The most we can hope for is not sure understanding but rather grateful receptivity to the advent of the Light. Here we are, preacher and congregation in Advent darkness, as if standing upon a hillside at evening, gazing up at shooting stars, watching a grand divine performance, listening to the preacher comment from time to time on its brilliance.

The preacher admits that "one *could certainly ask whether it is really true* that the Savior has kindled such a light in the world." Yet the preacher has little concern for our questions about God's truth. It is God who interrogates *us*, "Can what I have spoken become true among you?" It is not we who cross-examine God; God questions us. He is "calling us to account, . . . asking us what we have made of the light that has long since been given us at Christmas. And now it is up to us to give answer to God." Sometimes our debates among ourselves about God's truth are just another sinful means of evading the claims of truth, keeping truth abstract and theoretical rather than being God's truth for us. This truth is not that which is only to be assented to; we must also be "standing on it and making it valid in our thoughts, words, and acts."

Again, I believe the preacher's point that the light shines into the world, our world, and that the light ought to make a difference in our darkness—all this would be more engagingly made if the preacher had been willing to specify where and how in our time and place, in our darkness, this glorious light shines.

December 25, 1918

Luke 2:25–32

Now there was a man in Jerusalem whose name was Simeon; this man was righteous and devout, looking forward to the consolation of Israel, and the Holy Spirit rested on him. It had been revealed to him by the Holy Spirit that he would not see death before he had seen the Lord's salvation. Guided by the Spirit, Simeon came into the temple; and when the parents brought in the child Jesus, to do for him what was customary under the law, Simeon took him in his arms and praised God, saying, "Master, now you are dismissing your servant in peace, according to your word; for my eyes have seen your Savior, whom you have prepared in the presence of all peoples, a light to illumine the Gentiles and for glory to your people Israel." (alt.)

1. To celebrate Christmas means to see *salvation*. The birth of Jesus was its *beginning*, its dawn, its coming. Here was only the infant and not yet all the great and wonderful things that would go forth and unfold from this child, who came into the world so that the world might become new. Yet in the child Jesus the *new world* itself was already present; in the beginning was the end; in the seed, the certain guarantee of the coming fruit. Not a half of something, nor something partial and imperfect, but complete salvation, the salvation that God prepares for and gives the world, is present in the child. To celebrate Christmas means to *see* salvation. It means *no longer only to believe* in Christmas, not only to hope for it and to wander toward it in the dark night, but to see it. The shepherds could go to Bethlehem and see what the Lord had made known to them [Luke 2:15]. It was given to the aged Simeon to see salvation in the temple. This seeing too has to do with something present and tangible, with having and possessing something real.

Empty wishing, seeking, and desiring do not belong to Christmas. No. The words of a hymn ["Warum sollt' ich mich denn grämen"] express just the opposite: "Lord, my shepherd, fountain of all joy, you are mine, I am yours, none can separate us. . . . You are mine, because I hold you, and never let you, my light, leave my heart!" This belongs to Christmas, not *closed doors*, unanswered questions, impassable ways, and unfulfilled hopes. To celebrate Christmas means precisely to see what we always only seek; it means to be allowed to take and use what we long for.

Unresolved *misunderstandings* do not belong to Christmas, and neither do hard and tense oppositions; nor do cares that we cannot bear and that no one helps us unburden; nor goodwill that never becomes act; nor evil and dangerous conditions that are left as they are, with no attempt to change them; nor misery inside and outside, for which there is no redeeming word; nor a dark world that, with a shrug of the shoulders, one lets go its own deplorable way; nor the death that one cannot see beyond. When Christmas happens, all that belongs to the past.

To celebrate Christmas means to see that all that is old, petrified, and dry begins to move and flow, and that *we* too, after long standing still, begin to move and develop in a new way. This is what the celebration of Christmas means: to see how God, with helping hands, takes the world and all of us on himself.

And when God acts, how can we be mere observers? How can we do otherwise than participate in what God is doing? To celebrate Christmas, dear friends, means to take part in a great *transformation*, a factual and decisive transformation of all things. It means to see the world, life, and ourselves with the *eyes of God*. It means to perceive *God's shining light* in the world, in life, and in ourselves [cf. John 1:5]. For both belong together: the eyes of God and God's light. Where both are, that is where *all is changed* and becomes new. What was hard becomes soft; what was petrified begins to move; what was unstable and unsure becomes firm and sure; the captive becomes free.

The hidden *love of God* is poured out like a flood, bringing salvation. *God's thoughts* about the world, as God thought them before we human beings disordered them in our lives, are again honored. *The joy* that is the being of all beings, God, can again break forth, after having been so long suppressed by our foolishness. Angels, whom shortsighted human understanding reduced to fairy tales, are once more over the earth and speak to human beings, and human beings no longer wish to be more clever than God, but instead add their voices to the angels' song of praise.

2. But who may and can celebrate Christmas in this way? Our text tells the story of a man who was both able and permitted to do so, which means it was given by God. His name was Simeon. It is said of him that he was a *righteous and pious* man. In his case these words have, as they do generally in the Bible, a particular meaning. If we were to explain them by saying that he was decent, honest, and of a Christian mind, we would have understood neither him nor the secret of the right celebra-

tion of Christmas. His righteousness and devoutness were not human qualities that, by themselves, would have distinguished him from other human beings. His righteousness and piety were rather quiet and hidden gifts and acts of God in him. And that is the point: God must do something to us if there is to be Christmas. Here we cannot take charge or make anything of Christmas based on ourselves and our initiative. Something must happen to us from God's side, and we must only let it happen willingly, in openness for it. It does not have at first the effect of making us better than other people, and it does not bestow any sort of distinction in the eyes of human beings. But it will create the possibility of seeing God's salvation. This possibility, this condition that only God creates in us, is what the Bible calls righteousness and piety.

Simeon "looked forward to the consolation of Israel." This consolation is *more than human* consolation, for here it is God who must prove God's promises true. When God does this, it is something whole, deep, and perfect, and it fills the earth. For God is God, and God cannot deceive, nor can God do anything halfway. Simeon *looked forward* to this great, coming consolation. He did not let himself be distracted by all the contrary evidence that seemed daily to contradict it. Nor could he *be content* with all the lesser things one hopes for, all of which are limited to a certain period of time. He looked beyond all that was provisional and limited, both the good and the bad, beyond happiness and unhappiness, *to the whole*. He *judged* all temporal relationships and events only in their relationship to this whole. In all temporality he saw something of the forward-moving *hand of the clock* that tells us that time passes in order to open us to eternity. Such looking forward does not belong to the abilities and arts of human being, but is a *divine work* in human being! Only God can make human beings so restless, so much without consolation, that in their hearts they become deeply *tired* of the present world; that they seek their consolation entirely in God's *future;* that no earthly, temporal *hindrance* can overcome their hope; that no *human consolation* can content them; and that no human thoughts and expectations can distract them from their goal. Only God can create in us such faithfulness in anticipating and in looking forward to God's salvation. The only thing that Simeon added of his own was that he obeyed the heavenly voice [cf. Acts 26:19].

But there was more. *The Holy Spirit had an eye on Simeon.* The Holy Spirit has *nothing to do with human virtue,* but is the personal power of God, and God wants to *send the Spirit from heaven down* to us, God's human children. No one can *take* this power for themselves, nor can one imitate it, although both have often been tried. But such attempts only demonstrate that there have been whole periods of history and entire communities, peoples, and provinces to whom the Spirit could not descend from heaven, because their guilt was a hindrance. At the time of Simeon, for several centuries the people of Israel had not received the Holy Spirit, although God ever again had an eye on individuals, especially those who *persistently looked forward* to what God would do in the future. It is as if God said to each of these individuals, "*You* will experience something new! You will see it! In your place, in your time, and in your particular way, you will be an instrument of God." And where the Holy Spirit claims someone in this way, there one may assume that great *manifestations* of God are near, manifestations that will be given not just to certain individuals but to many. What individuals like Simeon are given to experience through the Spirit, through this personal power of God, always stands *in connection* with what afterward many will experience. It makes a way, so to speak, for the great deeds of God. Together with several others, Simeon was such a person *marked* by the Spirit. He was marked by *God's choice* and not by any choice of his own. In all human relations we can choose and act to take up what we will, but in relationship to the kingdom of God and to its quiet way through the world, *we are* chosen. What we can do is only to ensure that we are *open*, that we do not have deaf ears that cannot hear, when the *fire of Spirit* comes near to us. Simeon had done that.

And now what is most remarkable: "*It had been revealed to him* by the Holy Spirit that he would not see death before he had seen the Lord's salvation." We see again and very clearly how absolutely elevated the relationship was that such individuals had to God, and how it very much exceeds what we call righteousness and piety. He had been given instruction, like one might receive a command from a king. His life had been placed in a very definite order; there could be no hesitation, no deliberation, and no doubting, but only obedience. Here was something like the heavenly compulsion that compelled the old prophets, Abraham, Moses, Isaiah, Jeremiah. It later compelled John the Baptist too, even if he had wanted to act differently. Out of this heavenly compulsion, out of this divine captivity, came Simeon's faithful looking forward to the consolation of Israel; and so also the Holy Spirit could be inclined to him as a friend to a friend. *We,* on the other hand, are used to dealing with God from case to case, always with the questions, "Should I do it? Do I want to do it? Do I not want to do it?" *There are persons,* like Simeon, for whom this dubious kind of freedom is at an end. God has become too strong for them [cf. Jer. 20:7], and now they must order their lives completely according to their relationship to God. All their thoughts move more and more in one direction, and everything that could separate them from their relationship to God becomes more and more impossible. If we should once receive such a revelation, such information from God, we would be in the same situation. Not long would we then be proud of our own freedom, or of the way we swing now this way, now that way, in the exercise of this our human freedom. Simeon received information from God, and he had no choice but to keep to what it told him to do.

Now for the astonishing content of this information: there will be a miraculous triumph over death. Simeon was told that he would not die until he had seen the Lord's salvation, the promised consolation of Israel. *We all,* in some way or other, hope for consolation and redemption. But when we do so, we have the idea that first we have to die. As a poem says, "The pilgrim finds peace only when covered by the grave." It is only beyond death that we expect heaven, so it is no wonder that our hope is often so weak and unsure. How should we know that there is a heaven after death, when this side of death we expect nothing of heaven? The shadow of death lies on our hope and makes it and everything else doubtful. It was *different* for Simeon. For him the reality was very clearly and very explicitly this: First live, then die! First eternity, then the end of temporal life! First the Lord Christ, then the lord death!—only now death is no longer the lord who makes the eternal uncertain, but the enemy bound and tied; death can no longer put an end to our life, but as a servant it must do its service to us. First the full gleam of the morning light of eternity, the full glory of God beaming into these breakable, mortal, earthly dwellings [cf. 2 Cor. 5:1], and only then their collapse and death—a death that can have no claim on those who presently, as once Simeon did, live in these mortal dwellings.

But this was not all. Simeon *accepted* this information and subjected himself to it. It held him in *expectant* anticipation, made him able to begin each day with new hope, and made every day fruitful in what he did. This was the divine *compulsion,* the divine captivity that held him. In the words of Psalm 118:15–18: "There are glad songs of victory in the tents of the righteous: 'The right hand of the LORD does valiantly. . . . I shall not die, but I shall live, and recount the deeds of the LORD. The LORD has indeed disciplined me, but he did not give me over to death" (alt.). Is it necessary for me to say that *this revelation, this information from above,* came from God, just as everything the Holy

Spirit does is a work from above? If it were possible for Simeon, from here below, to form such an understanding of life out of himself, why are there not more persons with this remarkable understanding of life? Simeon made nothing himself, but he did *recognize* something, and he willingly recognized it. He was not unteachable, but someone who could be instructed about the coming of the truth.

3. People like Simeon are those who can and may celebrate Christmas. *What is Christmas for them other than* the divine answer to their whole life? This answer is given to them just as certainly as the question itself is not their own invention, but is raised in their hearts by God. We clearly see a reflection of the splendor of the Savior in the faces of the fathers and prophets of Israel who expectantly looked forward to his coming. How much more must a great light have illuminated Simeon and John the Baptist, who stood so near to the historical life of Jesus Christ? Wherever there was a person like Simeon—a righteous and pious person not according to the world, but according to the meaning given these words by the Bible—that person stood certainly also in the light of God and was in some way given the gift of seeing salvation and celebrating Christmas. In most cases such persons will have been completely unknown and hidden from recognition by the world, as was Simeon himself. Perhaps we all live, far more than we are aware, from the fact that such persons—those for whom Christmas really can happen—have never been completely missing from the world. Through them, in spite of all darkness, the divine and eternal has always remained to some small degree at home here on the earth. For their sake the angels have never completely ceased to sing of honor to God in the highest, of peace on earth, and of persons with whom God is well pleased [Luke 2:14].

Yes, I would go yet further and say: *Wherever human beings* have been *given to see* even a little of God's salvation; wherever *Christmas has really been celebrated* in homes and communities, in churches and among peoples and nations; wherever human beings have been given to see something of *the light of God* with the *eyes of God*—all this has happened because something of Simeon's way of being was in them, something of that looking forward to the consolation of Israel. It happened because, as with Simeon, the eye of the Holy Spirit was on them, and that divine message was given them that says, "First live, then die; first Christ this side of death, then death!" *There is joy because* of those who have been given to say, "My eyes have seen your salvation!" They can

honestly *test themselves* by the model of Simeon and ask whether they
have deceived themselves, whether they may really think and speak in
this way! Ever again *they seek this one source,* God, so that in the future
they may and can see salvation, and in ever richer, fuller measure. This
must again be emphasized: *Only as the answer to a life like Simeon's,* a
way of being like Simeon's, can Christmas be celebrated in truth.

It is something great to be given to say, "Master, now dismiss your
servant in peace!" After *looking forward in anticipation and expectation,*
something new enters in, namely what was expected, but only where it
really was expected. There is an outpouring of the Holy Spirit, but only
where the Spirit is able to come near to human being, as a friend comes
near to a friend. There is a *dissolving of that compulsion* and captivity in
which God holds us: the divine binding that held the prophets is not
the final and the highest relationship to God that God wills for human
beings. But this dissolving can only take place where we first truly experience and bear within us that first compulsion of God's Spirit. How
should God will to dismiss us in peace as long as we have not in the
least been God's servants, but have rather shortsightedly and defiantly
insisted on our own thoughts and our own ways? The dawn of the *day
of salvation can* only happen where the difficult and quiet work of Simeon has really been done. But this should not frighten us, for it is rather
meant as an invitation.

For the work of Simeon is not a bold venture of a human being based
on self, no enthusiastic human striving, no feat of difficult thought or
preparation for such a feat. All such requirements would receive the
very human response, "I cannot do that, that is too difficult, I do not
understand it." No, it is a work of God, a work that God does in us.
And God *wants to do this work* in us. God wills to begin with each of us
exactly at the point where each of us now stands. It is if God said to each
of us in turn: "You begin in your small *circle of life,* and you in your
large, socially important circle! You keep more to your *church,* and you
to your separatist chapel; and you, if you prefer, go to neither! You read
more in the Bible, and you, if you think it helps you, read more in the
newspaper! You be a liberal, and you a socialist!" In comparison with
what is most important, all of these are secondary and can be dealt with
later. They are things every individual has to decide *for oneself;* and each
will find the needed solution, if a person is honest and upright! But
what is most important is this: *be like Simeon. Do not resist,* when God
wills to do a work in you too, and *be mindful* that God can do more
in you than ever before. As we wait for and hasten toward the coming

day of the Lord [cf. 2 Pet. 3:12], we do *not* want to *avoid* it, for we all hunger and thirst to see the salvation of God. If *we* do not turn aside, God will *not turn aside* from us. And if today we have recognized for the first time what it means to hasten willingly and joyfully toward the great God, and if there is in us only a *small, timid beginning* of becoming like Simeon, truly we are *not far* from, but very near the moment when the light of Christmas will ascend brightly over us, when we will joyfully join our voices in the refrain "Christ the Savior is born!"

COMMENTS

"It was given to the aged Simeon to see salvation." The light that was heralded last Sunday now copiously breaks through in Barth's jubilant Christmas sermon, shining first on an old man who holds a baby in his arms, then shining upon us. "It was given to the aged Simeon to see salvation."

"To celebrate Christmas means to see *salvation*." Salvation is no longer a contested notion, a dim possibility. "Not *closed doors*, unanswered questions, impassable ways, and unfulfilled hopes"; rather, salvation as present, world-changing reality. This insight proved crucial for future Barthian theology. Everything that needs to be done for us has been done. The work of salvation is fully accomplished. We bask in the light of that finished work of God. We have no mountain to ascend to salvation; as Jesus said from the mountain of Calvary, "It is finished." The preacher therefore need not, through the sermon, argue, plead, artfully move a congregation somewhat closer to God, or commend a way that has yet to be trod; the preacher announces what God has done and invites the congregation to live in the light of the triumphant word: "It is finished."

True, we are not yet fully in this new world, and that is the baffling question of our predicament. Why, in God's name, do we refuse to live in the light of the accomplished facts? "Yet in the child Jesus the *new world* itself was already present; . . . the certain guarantee of the coming fruit. Not a half of something, nor something partial and imperfect, but complete salvation, the salvation that God prepares for and gives the world, is present in the child." Most of us probably think of a baby as a beginning, a human being in miniature, a potential adult. This baby is a sign of God's decisive, complete, full salvation. There is nothing in this Christmas gospel for us to do, think, or feel. We are to be like old Simeon—simply receive the babe who is given to us. As Simeon takes the babe in his aging arms, we are taken into God's arms: "Christmas means: to see how God, with helping hands, takes the world and all of us on himself."

Christmas is not a sweet feeling, a projection of the highest human aspiration. It is nothing less than "a factual and decisive transformation of all things." An evocative aspect of the Barthian theology of the atonement is that the incarnation fully contains the reconciliation of humanity to God. Christmas is as decisive in our redemption as Calvary. Thus, Barth manages to tie cross and resurrection, death and life to the Nativity in reading this story as "a miraculous triumph over death. Simeon was told that he would not die until he" sees the salvation of Israel. That promise is fulfilled even as the old man looks upon the baby Jesus. Even as early as the Nativity, "It is finished."

At Christmas, the gifted quality of our salvation is particularly manifest. Yet even Simeon's insight into the identity and significance of the baby is "given by God." If any of us are able to see the gift of Light at Christmas, that too is gift.

> God must do something to us if there is to be Christmas. Here we cannot take charge or make anything of Christmas based on ourselves and our initiative. Something must happen to us from God's side, and we must only let it happen willingly, in openness for it. It does not have at first the effect of making us better than other people, and it does not bestow any sort of distinction in the eyes of human beings. But it will create the possibility of seeing God's salvation.

Here Barth is the *sola fidei* Lutheran. What better time than Christmas to remind us that if we believe, if we see, if we understand, and if we follow—it is grace, all grace all the way down. Salvation is a name for who God is and what God does; it is not a word that denotes something to which we must assent or to which we need to contribute. "*The Holy Spirit had an eye on Simeon. The Holy Spirit has nothing to do with human virtue,* but is the personal power of God, and God wants to *send the Spirit from heaven down* to us, God's human children. No one can *take* this power for themselves, nor can one imitate it, although both have often been tried." We preachers must guard ourselves against the bane of self-help, auto-salvation techniques that attempt to pass themselves off as salvation. The gospel is never what we should, ought, or must do; it is what God has done, is doing, will do in Christ. All that is needed is the invitation to come, see our salvation.

Nothing much happens in any of Barth's sermons, no drama, few surprises, or artful use of narrative. Nothing needs to happen. Everything has already happened.

January 1, 1919

Psalm 23

The LORD is my shepherd, I shall not want. He makes me lie down in green pastures; he leads me beside still waters; he restores my soul. He leads me in right paths for his name's sake. Even though I walk through the darkest valley, I fear no evil; for you are with me; your rod and your staff—they comfort me. You prepare a table before me in the presence of my enemies; you anoint my head with oil; my cup overflows. Surely goodness and mercy shall follow me all the days of my life, and I shall dwell in the house of the LORD my whole life long.

1. The times are long past when we cross over into the New Year with pleasant and contented greetings and mutual good-luck wishes. The world now has a serious countenance, as those who are attentive are aware. Persons who live not just for themselves and in their own small circle, but who in a broad sense suffer the problems of the time—such persons go today into the New Year *full of concern.* Indeed they go into it with greater care than in the last year of the war. Now the war is over, and for this reason we could perhaps for a moment be less concerned.

But now one has to deal with balancing accounts regarding who was at fault for causing it, the evil it produced, and what we have learned or not yet learned. Attentive persons recognize that the prospects for this balancing of accounts are not good. The air above us is full of signs of coming storms; the ground trembles beneath us, announcing the coming of serious earthquakes. There are moments when one almost *envies* those who stand in the midst of these problems and must repent for the sins of the past. I think, for example, of the unfortunate country Russia. I also think of the deeply humiliated German people. What stands before the *rest of us:* before those who with the air of righteousness savor the victory, or before those who are merely observers? Like the old Russia and the old Germany, we in our own way have believed in the forces that brought about the war and the revolution: we have believed in money; in an only outward culture without the cultivation of the person; in a Christianity that is nothing more than decoration; in the might of the military; in social prejudices. Who believes more in these things than the English, the Americans, the Swiss? In some places the house that was built on these basic principles has collapsed in fear and suffering. I remember the words of the Hungarian government official István Tisza, murdered in October of last year: "It *had* to happen!" Are the perverted principles on which we have built everything better able to bear the load in Switzerland than where the collapse is being suffered? It will also happen, as it must, in England and in France, and it will happen here. World history is uncannily consistent and conscientious; it forgets nothing and reveals what is concealed. What humanity sows, it must reap [cf. Gal. 6:7].

The thought of what will happen in the future must be alarming for those who know this. Not even with the most optimistic view of things can one say that in the past several months the victors in this war have sown *good seeds*. The same is to be said of us Swiss. We have learned very, very little. It may be that the vanquished in the war are far in advance of us in the rethinking and relearning that are now necessary. With astonishing certainty and self-justification, we Swiss are travelling *farther on the same roads* that led to the world war. We are astonishingly at ease in the confidence that what has been, with all its idols, can continue into eternity. The price will have to be paid for that. Serious persons are aware and are concerned. Not rest and quiet are to be expected, but rather new disturbances; not peace and understanding, but new oppositions; not the dissolution of tensions, but new and difficult problems and sufferings. Apparently we want all this, and in any case we have it: we are choosing the way of old Russia and of old Germany. In some way or other, and at some time or other, we will have to share their fate. For God will not be mocked [Gal. 6:7].

2. My friends, it is something exalted and powerful to read, hear, speak and apply to our lives the *words of the Twenty-third Psalm*, "The LORD is my shepherd . . ."—if we only *could*, if it were only permitted us! If we were allowed to grasp this wonderful comfort, this fullness of promise in the midst of this dark time! If we were allowed to say: "Yes, God will not be mocked. World history is the judgment of the world, and what must come, will come. But we, our people, our community, our congregation today—we turn and look with courage and hope into the future. We say the LORD is my shepherd . . ."

But we may not speak these words so easily. We may not spare ourselves the recognition that they are *not suited* to our mouths. The comfort and promise that shine forth in them are *fruits* that must first grow, and it is questionable whether this fruit has grown in us. It is questionable whether we may stand where we do and *at the same time* refer the words of the Twenty-third Psalm to ourselves. It is questionable whether the words of the psalm are suitable for us as *words for the beginning of the New Year. I do not say* that this is impossible. God has not closed the door, not for anyone among us. But none among us has, simply and immediately, *the right* to think that one can and may look as courageously and hopefully into the future as it is described in the psalm. *No one* can or may do that, including me myself and all those who are more serious and pious than I am. It is a very *foolish* thing to misuse the Bible for the purpose of deceiving ourselves about *our* situation. Whether we may apply the words to ourselves is highly questionable.

For first of all we must confess that *we all are caught up in the development* that now, so it seems, drives inexorably toward judgment: all of us, including the pastor and prominent, pious, and well-meaning persons. We stand on the side of the *old time:* Our interest and our happiness lie in ensuring that everything stays the same as it was before the war. *We aid and abet* the powers of the old time when we continue to give them our *respect;* when we constantly *yield* to them; when we speak where we should be *silent,* and are silent where we should *speak.* We *affirm* and strengthen what should quietly disappear, and we are *horrified* about things today that we should quietly understand. We are not with our *hearts,* love, and prayers involved in what is coming to be, but in what is passing. In our inmost being we have not yet recognized what is really happening. We have not yet heard the *call to repentance* that in our time is required of all humanity. And this "not yet" stands between us and the Twenty-third Psalm.

One can say, "The LORD is my shepherd," when one is on the other side of the ditch that we have not yet leaped over, on the other side of one's own inner upheaval, rethinking, relearning, even refeeling. Those who can truly say, "The LORD is my shepherd," have *made that leap.* They have *not resisted* God, who judges the world, but thrown themselves into God's arms and become God's captives. They have *not swum with the current of opinion* in the world, but against it. In them something has *turned* from the idols to God; they have *submitted* to judgment; they have let the *truth* rule in their hearts. They have at least inwardly separated themselves from the powers of the old world, when they were outwardly not yet superior to those powers. They have begun at least *to think differently,* to look in a different direction. And this is why they have been able, without exaggeration or presumption, to pray, "The LORD is my shepherd . . ." It was *true* for them. But for us it is not simply and immediately true, for it is not simply and immediately certain that we are and want to be participants in this process of transformation.

The words of the psalm speak to us today both as a *question* and as a *challenge*. They say, "Enter *into* this transformation! Become a *persistent*, recognizing, understanding person, a person who has *turned* from the idols to God, who can and may speak with the words of the psalm! Become a person who is being *renewed* and therefore has the faculty necessary for the courage and hope that we need so much today." Are you a person in transformation? And if you are not, do you realize that you must *become* such a person, so that you do not stand perplexed and without consolation in the situation of today's world? And if you do realize this, *what are you doing* about it? Dear friends, who among us has *no need at all* to ask this question? Who among us might venture impudently *to reach for* the divine fruit of comfort and promise without becoming a person in transformation? For this fruit is meant only for such persons. Do we not recognize that we would be lying to God if we said the words of the Twenty-third Psalm without becoming a person in renewal and transformation?

3. I can *imagine someone today* who is becoming such a person. Oh, if one of us could stand up and say, "I am such a person! Now let me tell you how I think about the future." This person would speak with us like this:

Yes, as I go into the New Year, *I too am burdened with serious cares and concerns*. I do not see the world through rose-colored glasses. I do not think people are better than they are. I know that for all guilt the penalty must be and is paid. I except from this guilt neither myself, nor my family, nor my country. I anticipate difficult, serious, and confused times to come for me and my children. I no longer rely on my small amount of money, nor on what is now called law and order, nor on my good intentions, nor on the goodwill of those around me. I know that we live in a time when everything is unstable: churches, states, the crowns of kings. Even less stable is the small frame of rights and duties that has until now held and protected me.

But in all this *I perceive the hand of God*, and certainly God's hand of judgment, which perhaps touches a great deal that is dear to me, and yet it is God's hand and not the hand of the devil. Whatever may fall under God's judgment must fall under it, and it will involve me as it must; but *God is dearer to me* than all else that is dear to me. In good times I forgot God long enough; I do not intend to lose God anew in evil times. *I understand God*, and I want to understand God. I see God pronounce judgment, because God will reveal God's *grace* on earth. I see God destroy, because God wills to *build*. I hear God say "No," in order that God's great "*Yes*" can be heard again. My *hope* is in God, and therefore I am *safe* in the middle of the storm. I look *forward to and await* God's light, and therefore all the darkness of the present can have *no* power over me. "The LORD is my shepherd, I shall not want. He makes me lie down in green pastures; he leads me beside still waters; he restores my soul." Yes, we can *sigh and yet still be blessed*.

In the tumult of this world I am *alone and almost always perplexed*. It is a bitter experience that I find only *few persons* around me with whom I can reach an understanding about what must be said and done. There are so few with whom one can seriously *work* and pray, so few that are a real *help* and in whom one can find good counsel. *I myself* am full of error and sin; I *stumble* like one who is not old enough to realize what he is doing. *I almost never know* what to do and how to go about it, so that I might oppose something really new and better to the suffering heart of the world. All the dams that I erect against the flood rip apart like the dams everyone else builds. Ever again I choose the wrong means; I do poor work; I do not hear God's word; I disrupt God's friendly intention; and *along with the world*, I make myself *guilty* again and again.

But there is one thing that does not let me go: *God speaks* to me. There is a *wisdom* in me—not my own wisdom nor a wisdom of other persons, but something of the wisdom of God. I have a feeling for what is right, and although I am often untrue to it, it is never untrue to me. It is a *light within me*, and when I have followed it, I have never wished I had not. From it I receive very definite directions: "Now left! Now right! Now straight forward!" And when I obey them, there is light in the tumult of the world and ground under my feet, so that something new does happen, something valuable, something that proves itself. Often I have the impression that I am only an *instrument* in what I do and say, so that I have the impression that I am under an inner compulsion! And this is a consolation for me, something that no one can take from me. I see something similar here and there *in another person*, as ships in the night see the lights of other ships. It is as if I were traveling somewhere, and *many* others, perhaps very many, were going with me, but I could not see them. I am glad when I occasionally *greet* one of these fellow pilgrims. So I am *not alone*, not abandoned. "He leads me in right paths for his name's sake. Even though I walk through the darkest valley, I fear no evil; for you are with me; your rod and your staff—they comfort me."

On this path I am tempted on all sides. *I too am earnestly a child* of this dark and guilty time, this dark and guilty world. Others are rightly *offended* at my failures and at all the things I have neglected. I have more than one *weak side*. And beyond this, I must suffer because I am right, because I am the mouthpiece and instrument of God, because of my task. This is no child's play; the task given by God is vulnerable in this world. *Much can be said*, based on a thousand reasons and experiences, against the venture of risking one's life with God, a venture in defiance of all those reasons and experiences. *Much can be held against* a person who has only one argument, only one proof, only one triumph: the quiet and peaceful divine truth. *Much can be done* to one who depends only on God. I stand there like a defenseless *child* in the middle of a battleground. I cannot refute them or hit them back or kill them, even if I wanted to.

But in all of this, *the experience has never left me*, and never will, that I am *protected* and that those who are against me cannot win out over me. Bad things can happen to me, but I will *not be overcome*. I can become the object of mocking and laughter, but I am the one who can first laugh to the point of tears. All of that is true because my life is *not mine*, and my task is *not mine*. For me to be completely overcome, God would have to no longer be God; but that cannot happen. One can frighten and harass me, but what can it accomplish, when there is something in me that is not me? God is not afraid. God in heaven laughs at them [cf. Ps. 2:4]. Do what you can to me, try your best; in all of what you may do, I hope and I know that *something in me* will remain calm and will not fall to temptation. "You prepare a table before me in the presence of my enemies; you anoint my head with oil; my cup overflows."

I also know that I am *human and have a short life*, that one day I must die, and perhaps very soon. *What then am I?* Will I enjoy *success* before my death? Will I *see a ray of light* from the dawn of the coming kingdom of God? Will I in dying be able to be clearly right about something over against those who just flow with the stream? Will I ever have the joy of finally being recognized as right? Very probably not; no, emphatically not. I know that I must be ready *to do without any success*. And I know that it is the highest possible honor to be included among those in the book of life, about whom it is said in Hebrews 11:39 that "*all these*, though commended for their faith, did not receive what was promised." If it pleases my cleverer children, may they write sardonically on my gravestone: Here lies one who dreamed and deceived himself!

And yet over and above all of this, I know that *my small life is not in vain*. I say this again for the reason that it is *no longer my life*: it is taken captive and sold to God. *What belongs* to God is not in vain. God builds God's eternal kingdom out of many such combative pilgrim lives. They are *the instruments of the grace* that breaks through the darkness of judgment. The others too, including those who unthinkingly flow with the stream, live now, already, from these instruments of grace. If there were not such persons, such instruments of grace, life would be intolerable. *It is enough for me* to be thankful for that highest possible and undeserved honor of being included among those whose names are written in the book of life [cf. Rev. 17:8]. It is enough that God *uses* me for God's purposes and that many, without knowing it, *are nourished through me.* It is enough that, even though it is inconceivable, I may be a little salt in the world [cf. Matt. 5:13]. The salt may disappear, but its penetrating effect remains. Whether I live or die, in the hand of God I do not die, for God is not a God of the dead [Mark 12:27 par.]. "Surely goodness and mercy shall follow me all the days of my life, and I shall dwell in the house of the LORD my whole life long." I will live into the dark and unknown future as one consoled, courageous, and full of hope.

4. Dear friends, imagine that we could *hear a person say all that.* Please understand that I am not saying that I *arrogate to myself* the right to say it. I have said it not in my name, but in the name of the Twenty-third Psalm. As far as I am concerned, I would only add that I wish I could speak like that. It is true, is it not, that *we all wish* the same thing. For we sense that it would be the ideal attitude for facing the New Year and all future times happily and as sincere and upright persons. There would be neither rose-colored glasses nor dark pessimism. We would be calm, brave, honest, and certain that things would be made right. For when we are certain that God is coming, we are certain that things will be made right. Please understand that I am not saying, *"Therefore let us speak like the Twenty-third Psalm."* That would be but another churchly deception, and we have no intention of closing this sermon with it. For the question is precisely whether or not we *may so speak.* Neither for you nor for me do I *answer* the question. However, I do want to close with reference to the fact that we may so speak. *In Christ,* in view of the change that has occurred through him, in obedience to him, and in spite of the darkness that still fills the earth, we may so speak. Christ has *not been born in vain.* He has rather been born so that the Twenty-third Psalm can be true even for us. But now we stand before the *question of all questions,* before the deepest and most burning *question of the time.* It is the question that, like no other, rules and determines the New Year and all the future: whether or not we will be

able to say, with the old Simeon in the temple, that our eyes have *seen* the salvation of God [cf. Luke 2:30].

COMMENTS

No cheerful "Happy New Year!" in Barth's 1919 New Year's sermon. Here Barth has as much to say about current events in the world as in any of his early sermons. The Great War has at last dragged on to a ragged ending. One might think that the preacher would see a rosy New Year. But no, dark new forebodings grip the preacher. Now is the time for deep concern rather than facile celebration. "The air above us is full of signs of coming storms; the ground trembles beneath us, announcing the coming of serious earthquakes." Don't think that we are over and done with the war; the sins of our past are yet with us. "World history is uncannily consistent and conscientious; it forgets nothing and reveals what is concealed." One almost envies the defeated Germans and the miserable Russians. They sense, better than we Swiss, trying to stand at a distance, the miserable moral failure of the war. At least no German congregation needs be told that the coming year will not be happy. "Not rest and quiet are to be expected, but rather new disturbances; not peace and understanding, but new oppositions."

In his gloomy assessment of the coming year, Barth is trying to teach his congregation to think providentially: "in all this *I perceive the hand of God*, and certainly God's hand of judgment, which perhaps touches a great deal that is dear to me, and yet it is God's hand and not the hand of the devil." One reason we come to church is to discern the signs of the times theologically. Our times, the uncertainty and foreboding that we face, are actually gifts from "God's hand" rather than simply a bad period of world history. What we may think at first to be a time of disorder and dissolution is, in reality, a time when the Shepherd leads, even if we are being led into territory where we don't want to go.

I wonder how many Swiss congregations were being told that they, as much as the English, Germans, and French, were responsible for this pointless war?

> Like the old Russia and the old Germany, we in our own way have believed in the forces that brought about the war and the revolution: we have believed in money; in an only outward culture without the cultivation of the person; in a Christianity that is nothing more

than decoration; in the might of the military; in social prejudices. Who believes more in these things than the English, the Americans, the Swiss?

I marvel at a preacher so tethered to the Word that he could make that statement to his Swiss congregation. Then again, I'm in the moderate, mainline American church who, when asked by our president to get in line behind the flag and support the war effort in Iraq, of all places, lacked the theological resources to say "No!"

The preacher admits that talk of repentance is not easy, particularly coming from a preacher who also needs to repent. "I must suffer because I am right, because I am the mouthpiece and instrument of God, because of my task. This is no child's play; the task given by God is vulnerable in this world." Thus, I marvel at Barth's God-induced homiletical courage, courage all too rare among us contemporary preachers, or at least in short supply in me.

Yet the preacher acknowledges his own consolation, even in his obedient fulfillment of his "task given by God." "Over and above all of this, I know that *my small life is not in vain*. I say this again for the reason that it is *no longer my life*: it is taken captive and sold to God." A preacher who is captive to God, whose life is not one's own, whose words have been commandeered by God, is marvelous to behold.

About a fourth of the way into his sermon, Barth finally mentions his text: the Twenty-third Psalm. I confess that I don't think that this sermon has very much to do with this biblical text. I have no idea what Barth means when he urges us to become persons "in renewal and transformation," and I cannot figure out how he got that out of this text. If the preacher wants to speak about repentance, one thinks of dozens of better texts with which to urge repentance.

As I hear him, the preacher openly announces that he will *not* preach on the peaceful and reassuring Psalm 23 because there is no way that people like us—self-contented, self-righteous Swiss that we are—can receive the consolation of this psalm. "We have not yet heard the *call to repentance* that in our time is required of all humanity. And this 'not yet' stands between us and the Twenty-third Psalm."

While I am unsure that the preacher demonstrates that the Twenty-third Psalm is in fact a call to repentance, Barth's angle here is interesting. Some biblical texts can be understood only through repentance, through moral transformation that makes us capable readers of Scripture. The peace, reassurance, and consolation to be had through the declaration, "The LORD is my shepherd . . ." are not given to those for whom the Lord is not their shepherd. Having followed "too much the devices and desires of our own hearts," as the Book of Common Prayer once put it, we are far removed from the trusting assurance of Psalm 23. We who "walk through the darkest valley" are destined to walk alone because that's the way we want it. In glibly saying, "The LORD is my shepherd," "do we not recognize that we would be lying to God?"

The only way for this Scripture to work for us is for it to work in us. Elsewhere Barth said that every passage of Scripture ought to be read as vocation, as a summons from God. In interpreting Scripture, understanding is always dependent upon obedience. Forsaking all our false gods who led us into this disaster of a war and its aftermath, let us repent, turn around, change our allegiance, and allow the Lord to shepherd us into a truly New Year. "'Surely goodness and mercy shall follow me all the days of my life, and I shall dwell in the house of the LORD my whole life long.' I will live into the dark and unknown future as one consoled, courageous, and full of hope."

Matthew 9:14–15

Then the disciples of John came to him, saying, "Why do we and the Pharisees fast often, but your disciples do not fast?" And Jesus said to them, "The wedding guests cannot mourn as long as the bridegroom is with them, can they? The days will come when the bridegroom is taken away from them, and then they will fast."

1. If we want to have a clear *picture of the Savior*, we must make the effort to understand who the Pharisees were, for in the New Testament they form the background of the picture of Jesus. We *cannot regard the Pharisees highly enough*, for their way was, in human terms, the best way that anyone can take. This is demonstrated very clearly by our text, where they are mentioned together with the *disciples of John the Baptist*, of whom Jesus said, "Among those born of women no one has arisen greater than John the Baptist" [Matt. 11:11]. This should keep us from having a low opinion of the Pharisees, from making the sign of the cross, so to speak, to forbid the thought that we ourselves might finally be Pharisees. The Pharisees stood *as high* on the scale of good, religious people as we can possibly imagine, and it is no dishonor at all for us to be Pharisees. They were indeed *enemies of the Savior*, but one can be an enemy of the Savior and in all seriousness still be a person that others should highly respect. If that is not clear to us, we will *never understand who Jesus Christ is* and what *he* has to say and give to us. We always think we have to make it very clear that *we too are good, religious people*. But we do not have to do this at all, because Jesus does not say that we are not good, religious people. If we really must have him confirm that we are good, he will. But it is such a pity that we always think Jesus *has nothing other to say and give to us* than what a good person knows and does anyway, because then we pass right by Jesus. The whole point with Jesus is that he says and brings more to us than the best and most

pious persons; he is more than John the Baptist. The gospel consists in this "*more than*," and this is where Christianity begins.

2. *John the Baptist* bowed before Jesus as the greater and more power-ful one who was to come [cf. Mark 1:7 par.]. John saw his own task as that of only *pointing to* the one who had more and better things to say and give than he did with his message of "repent and convert!" The *Pharisees*, for their part, did not bow to Jesus but *refused* him. They mistrusted him and warned others away from him, because they were *sure* of themselves and certain in *their way of being.* They thought they had already found the way of truth and life in their own thinking and striving for God and the good. Therein lies their enormous *difference* from Jesus.

Yet also for this reason, and as our text from Matthew says, the Phar-isees had *much in common* with the disciples of John. The Pharisees are, so to speak, *the relatives* of the prophets, certainly unequal relatives, but nevertheless relatives, members of a family. They have something of the inexorable earnestness of *Moses* and the consuming zeal of *Elijah.* They have something of the humble reverence for the holiness of God that was in *Isaiah*, and something of the interior, melancholic, pas-sionate love of God that lived in *Jeremiah.* And we can go even further and say that they had something of the defiant faith of *Luther,* of the holy rigor and conscientiousness of *Calvin;* and they had the energetic power of action that we find in *Zwingli.* One does no discredit to the most pious *preacher of the awakening,* or to the most heroic *missionary,* or to the most eager *friend of the people,* or to the most honorable *man of the church*, when the Pharisees are listed in the same series with them and they in the same series with the Pharisees. Even as he grew older the apostle Paul himself did not deny that he had been and still was a Pharisee [Acts 23:6 par.].

If one were to ask whether the Pharisees recognized their *sinfulness*, the answer would have to be that they *did* as well as any serious Chris-tian in our time. If one were to ask whether they were *converted,* the answer would be that they *were,* and so thoroughly as anyone of us who considers oneself converted. If one were to ask whether they prayed, the answer would be that prayer was one of the obligations that they were most exact and most serious about. If we wanted skeptically to ask whether they also did *good works,* they would probably shame every one of us, for they made their whole life into a work of piety and love of neighbor. If we ask whether the salvation of their fellow human beings was a heartfelt issue, the answer is that for them all that was honorable was directed to winning the godless and the heathen for God. It was no exaggeration when a Pharisee once said to Jesus, "Master, I have kept *all these commandments* since my youth" [cf. Mark 10:20 par.].

There is surely nothing great and difficult that one can ask of a person that the Pharisees were not *aware of* and did not *strive to accomplish*. In their *knowledge* of what is good and godly, in their *striving* for it, in their *serious and awakened* being, they were fully one with the disciples of John. But *their ways separated* when the light of Christmas dawned above them. They were deeply *different* in their attitude toward Jesus, which showed that there are *different kinds of being serious* and *different kinds of awakening*. Yet apart from their attitude toward the Savior, the prophets and the Pharisees went the *same good, laudable way*. Both were *Advent persons* who awaited the kingdom of God with all seriousness and prepared the way for it [cf. Mark 1:3 par.]. They had repentance, holiness, faith, love, and hope [cf. 1 Cor. 13:13]. *If only we were* on the serious path that they took!

3. As Jesus came with his disciples, he caused *deep disappointment,* great offense, and real pain to both the Pharisees and the prophets, *and to the disciples of John,* and perhaps to John himself. But however that may be, *John* got beyond the disappointment and offense and came to understand Jesus. A *number* of his disciples did not understand Jesus, and for many years after the death of Jesus, they formed their own community separate from the Christians. Some of this we can read about in Acts [18:25; 19:3]. Jesus presented a very great enigma to all those who went that good and praiseworthy path of the Pharisees and prophets, and the enigma is still here today. The Savior still presents an enigma that is a hindrance to understanding him. One can almost say that the more seriously, courageously, and *consciously a person follows the way* of the prophets and Pharisees, the greater the step becomes that one must take in order to come to Jesus.

4. But what was so hard to understand, what was so *enigmatic in the Savior*? In summary, it was this. The Pharisees and the disciples of John increasingly had the impression that the *Savior was not a pious person.* They had the most serious reservations about him precisely at the points that were for them sure and unquestioned. Did he take sin *seriously enough*? Was he truly a *converted* person? Did he have *sufficient respect for God*? Did he preach *repentance* to sinners *urgently* enough? Did he

do what was *required* of a serious-minded person? These reservations about Jesus were at times expressed with rough clarity, such as when they said that he committed blasphemy against God [Mark 2:7 par.], or that he was "a glutton and a drunkard, a friend of tax collectors and sinners" [Matt. 11:19 par.]. Often they concealed themselves behind the *veil* of many different cautious and mistrusting questions, such as we find on almost every page of the Gospels. They were always there, and they were the most difficult *hindrance* standing in the way of the Savior. So the most difficult hindrance lay not in the malice of worldly persons but in the righteousness of the children of God. Not the defiance of the godless, but the serious reservations of the awakened and converted brought him finally to the cross. We must clearly understand *this relationship* between the Savior and the Pharisees: to the pious he was not pious; to the serious he was not serious; to the converted he was not converted. Indeed, openly or secretly they straightway denied that he was honest and upright in what he said about God. John and his disciples let themselves be taught that this was not true, while the Pharisees persisted in their own understanding of Jesus. So strongly did they object to him that they finally wanted him dead and caused his death, something they never tried to do with even the worst of publicans. That was how terribly serious they were about the Savior not being a pious man.

5. This great mistrust was also expressed in the question of John's disciples about *why they and the Pharisees fasted so much, while Jesus and his disciples did not fast at all.* In those times fasting was one of the most important ways in which persons demonstrated that they were to be taken seriously. In these circles it was self-evident that on certain days and at certain times one freely made these sacrifices. It was supposed to be a kind of *gift* that one brought to God, or an act of *self-discipline,* or a *denial of self* to save money for the benefit of others, such as today in the Salvation Army's week of self-denial. Jesus did *not* take this fasting *seriously.* He did not forbid fasting to his disciples, but he also did not tell them to fast. In his doings it was as if this pious work did not exist. Perhaps it *surprises* us today that the Pharisees mistrusted him on this point, insofar as fasting has become something foreign for us Protestants. But in those times, for the right-minded, fasting was a *common* practice, perhaps comparable to the practice of paying one's dues as a member of a certain club, or giving thanks before eating, or attending church, or not knitting on Sunday. But while we do these rather as

sleepy habits, so to speak, in the time of Jesus practices such as fasting were done or not done far more consciously and zealously. But it was *not only at this point* that Jesus gave offense. For his disciples he also made *prayer* remarkably secret, something one should not talk about. When prayer did become public, it was not as it should be [cf. Matt. 6:5–8]. There was also little to hear or see of *their giving to charity* [cf. Matt. 6:1–4]. He and his disciples also transgressed against the commandment to keep the Sabbath holy, and they did so without having a bad conscience. Whether he observed the *love of country,* which at the time definitely belonged to religious piety, was more than doubtful.

Last Sunday we heard how he had no compunction about taking his disciples into notoriously *bad company* [Matt. 9:9–13]. Later there were even reports about very derogatory remarks he was supposed to have made about the *temple* in Jerusalem [cf. Mark 14:58 par.]. In short, it was hard to know what Jesus was doing, or rather, when all was taken together, one knew it all too well. Everywhere he said and did the *opposite* of what was expected of him as a promising young man of God. If one could excuse him for one thing or another, it was *impossible to overlook the whole* that lay behind all the single things he did and was evident in all of them: he lacked seriousness, repentance, decision, and clarity. On the day with which our text from Matthew is concerned, it was *fasting that stood in the foreground,* probably because Jesus had accepted an invitation to have dinner in the house of the publican [Matt. 9:10]. On another day it was something else that agitated these circles. But basically it was always *the same thing:* Jesus is *not* on the right path; one *cannot* take him seriously, one does *not* get to heaven on the way he leads his disciples; he is *not* a pious man.

6. How was the Savior to justify himself against such a harsh accusation? He answered with a parable: "The wedding guests cannot mourn as long as the bridegroom is with them, can they?"

What we first notice in this answer is the happy, cheerful picture in which he clothes it. If Jesus had been *upset* by the question asked of him in the text and by all the mistrust that lay behind it, he would have used entirely different words. But he was not upset. Imagine that it were said to one of us, "You act like you are serious, but truthfully you are not at all! You talk of God, and you do not even believe in God! You want to show others the way, and it is a completely wrong way!" If that were said to us, we would *recoil physically!* We would also find it necessary to consider whether what they said might finally be true! We would burst out against the one who attacked us and naturally use the words, "My conscience is clear!" We would not be calm at all but deeply disturbed. But Jesus *is calm*. From the very beginning he stands above the question and the accusation. One can almost say with certainty that when he gave his answer, he *smiled*, because he answered that *a marriage feast* was happening, a high time of celebrating, of being joyful, and that this was why his disciples did not fast. In this way Jesus could let the sun rise precisely at the moment they wanted to cast him into darkness.

The second remarkable thing in the parable of the marriage feast is that Jesus does *not justify* himself to his accusers. We are all artists in excusing ourselves when we are accused. The Savior too could have excused himself. He could also have told them that his disciples did *sometimes fast*, and that he himself had *fasted in the desert for forty days* [Mark 1:13 par.]. He might have said, "If we do not fast as much as you, we do other good works that you do not do and that are worth more than fasting." He could have referred to the fact that his disciples learned *a righteousness* from him that was better than that of the Pharisees and the disciples of John [cf. Matt. 5:20–48]. But he mentions *none of all that*. He does not enter into *competition* about who is more pious and more moral. He does *not defend* himself against the blow that strikes him. *He concedes,* it is true that by and large he and his disciples do not fast. And with this he silently concedes far more offenses to their way that they have not yet discovered. Effectively he admits that he is not pious, so that we can almost hear him say, "It is true, I am not a pious man!" And with cheerful words! He gives them a new reason to accuse him, for he shows that he can smile about the most serious things. In this way he defended himself by not defending himself; he compounded with new enigmas the enigma that so much offended them. And he needed no defense.

The third thing that is important in this answer is that he names what his accusers find missing in him: sadness, *mourning*. The wedding guests cannot mourn. Therefore *to fast is to mourn,* an obligation of those who sorrow, something one does for example at a funeral. In those circles this idea was certainly *something new*. As is said in the Sermon on the Mount [Matt. 6:16], those who fasted sometimes made a dismal face, but this was certainly not because they were sad. They were certainly conscious of fulfilling an obligation, and in doing so they perhaps put on a serious, important, official face, but they were not in mourning. They fasted with conviction, zeal, and *enthusiasm*. And now they heard from Jesus that their enthusiasm was in reality sadness, and that their fasting was mourning. The Savior had seen *deeply into* them, as only he sees into the human heart.

We can imagine him wanting to say to them:

Within you, seriousness and truth are *awakened;* you have heard God's call, and you have taken it on yourselves to be obedient. And you have become aware that you *need something that is now missing.* You see that you have taken on something enormously *difficult,* that you are involved in a *fight* that you are not equipped to win. You are never let go by what is of God: it is in front of you and beckons you, and it is behind you and pushes you. But always it is a *spur and prod* in your conscience and a high and distant *goal.* It is never power and love, but only law, like the air in which you live. *That is why you fast. That is why* the Sabbath is so important. *That is why* money burns your hand, so that you have to give to charity. *That is why* you are so very careful in fulfilling your obligation to prayer and belief. *That is why* you are so unrelenting, so avid, so conscientious, consuming everything in your zeal. *That is why* you are so serious and pious.

In the fine points you are very meticulous *because* you do not yet know the great gift that can now be given human beings. You bring God sacrifices *because* you have not yet experienced God's mercy. You prepare the way for the kingdom of God so avidly, with pick and shovel, *because* it has not yet come to you. *Because* you have not yet found the God you seek—that is why there must be prophets and Pharisees. (And we might also say, *because* it is not yet Christmas, it must be Advent, with all the seriousness and discipline that belongs to Advent.) Out of *this great affliction,* out of this *painful privation, come your fasting* and all the other things that are so important to you, and finally your damnation of me. Out of *humanity's great distress,* which knows only about human things, about its own will and exertion [cf. Rom. 9:16], but not about God's Savior, comes your *piety.* Oh, you may keep your opinion about your fasting, so go on, keep doing what you are doing as long as you must, but do not forbid others to go a different way because the affliction and the distress have been taken from them.

Here God's salvation has been victorious, and now bursts forth again *the great message and invitation;* with me and around me the joyous marriage feast is happening. Not that my disciples *would be better people* than you. We have no intention of competing with you, so let us not argue about that. But *here with me the distress* that oppresses you has been *done away with.* Here there is not only awakening but also *rising, getting up, and walking;* not only God's call but also *God's presence;* not only fighting but also *victory;* not only sacrifice but also the *mercy* that exceeds all understanding. Here is *God's kingdom*. Here there is *power and love;* here is *the divine as the air* in which one lives. Here nothing is lacking, nothing only sought, nothing only strived for, nothing only known, nothing only said. What no human has been able to say has here become an *event.* Here *God has helped human beings* and gives them what no human can give them.

Those who stand here stand on the *divine and heavenly side* of life. *That is why* they do not fast. *That is why* they do not have to be pious. *That is why* they may go a new way in a cheerfulness and freedom that is of God. *We do not come too near to you,* so you need not be concerned about us, and to you remains your fame: "Among all born of women no one has arisen greater than John the Baptist; *yet the least* in the kingdom of heaven is greater than he!" [Matt. 11:11, alt.; cf. German]. *Do not worry about us* as long as your own righteousness gives you no reason to worry about your-selves, as long as you do not recognize the dilemma and distress in which you stand. To know *God's mercy* is more than sacrifice [cf. Matt. 12:7], and *God's kingdom* is more than piety. Judge me as you will, but *do not impede the way* that I and those who belong to me must go; for here is more than Elijah. And if you ever recognize that God is with us, the God who makes an end to distress, then you will cease accusing me and instead join me in praising this God.

7. In our text Jesus adds something else, namely, these melancholy words: "The days will come when the bridegroom is taken away from them, and then they will fast." It will be a time and a condition in which the *distress and the privation* that oppressed the prophets and the Pharisees prevail again; it will be a time when, on the whole, nothing remains to *Christians themselves* but to go the way of the prophets and the Pharisees. Jesus very probably meant the time *in which we now live.* It is *an unnatural time,* for it is something unnatural, something strange, that the bridegroom is taken from the wedding guests as if by a violent theft. *Christianity is no longer* in the kingdom, in the power and love of God, as were the disciples of the Savior. An interim, *a great pause,* has come into being, delaying the joy that was then prepared for human beings. God has again become a stranger in the land [cf. Jer. 14:8]. That is why there *must now be many things* that belong neither to the Savior nor in Christianity, but to the Pharisees and the prophets.

Yet we want *at least to make an effort not to forget the Savior*—not to forget that *what is today called Christianity is not true Christianity,* no matter how beautiful it might be, but only a poor replacement. We want not to forget that *in truth we are not servants,* but called to the freedom of the children of God [cf. Gal. 5:13]. We want not to forget that there is something more serious than our greatest seriousness! And if we today, on the whole, must go the way of the Pharisees and the disciples of John, let us make a point of walking with those disciples of John who finally overcame their mistrust of the Savior. And let us not cease to ask and to plead that, after this long time of John the Baptist, a glorious and festive time of the Savior might come anew, a time that will bring not what human beings themselves can accomplish, but the joy and freedom that come from God and that descend from heaven with the Savior himself—that glorious and festive time that has been taken from us.

COMMENTS

By 1919 Barth's sermons sound as if the young preacher is finding his voice, as if he has increasing clarity and confidence about what he most wants to say. Unlike many of his early sermons, in this sermon Barth manages to maintain focus and tension throughout.

The interpretive key to this February 1919 sermon is Barth's strong opening assertion that the Pharisees must be viewed as thoroughly good, undeniably moral, sincerely pious people. The Pharisees stood at the summit of piety. The Pharisees were genuinely virtuous in every way—and they also happened to be "enemies of the Savior."

In *Romans* Barth presents a similar portrayal of the Pharisees, observing that our similarity to the Pharisees needs to be "repeated and listened to again and again" (100; see also 109). In our piety, morality, and fervent religiosity, *we* are the Pharisees. This contention saves this sermon from being anti-Jewish. Unlike some interpreters of his day, Barth doesn't criticize the Pharisees for being too zealously Jewish or deadly "legalistic"; rather, they are portrayed as just the sort of Swiss who might crawl out of bed and come to the village church to hear a sermon on a cold February morning.

The Pharisees were successful in being "religious," but the gospel is "more than" this. This "more than" is where Christianity begins. This surely is a message that is distinctively, relentlessly Barthian. Religion is paradoxical: under the guise of approaching God, religion is one of the most effective means of escaping God. Jesus presents the church with an insolvable enigma: "the more seriously, courageously, and consciously a person follows the way of the prophets and Pharisees, the greater the step becomes that one must take in order to come to Jesus." (I love that Barth relegates even the prophets to the ranks of the Jesus-hating Pharisees.)

"*The Savior was not a pious person.*" Barth, who was raised in a dedicatedly pious home, is fierce in his scorn for all piety, as his biographer has shown.[1] The greatest hindrance to Jesus, says Barth, was "not in the malice of worldly persons but in the righteousness of the children of God."

You want to see the work of the "children of God"? It was none other than the "awakened and the converted" who "brought him finally to the cross." Take that, church!

Because "he was *not* a pious person," Jesus didn't defend himself against the Pharisees' charge that he was impious. Jesus predicted a time of mourning in which we would have finally driven the Savior away with our sanctimonious piety. Listen, church, that mournful deadly unnatural time is now. The Pharisees have triumphed.

The sermon ends with a simple call to awake to our true situation, to accept the invitation to the party, to rise and respond to "not only God's call, but also *God's presence.*"

It seems to me that *presence* is the main thing here. The reason why the Pharisees (at least in this sermon) clung to their piety and criticized Jesus for his impiety was that their religiousness was a means of avoiding the claims of Christ present. The Pharisees (and we) have only one problem with God in Jesus Christ: God is *Jesus Christ.* Jesus was the undeniable presence of the God we hoped not to meet.

It is an enigmatic, counterintuitive thought that drives this sermon. In that, this sermon is counter to much preaching then and today. Many of today's better sermons say something well, but what they say well is nothing worth saying. Bad sermons tend to share a major flaw: they suffocate from a lack of interesting ideas. Barth's observations on Matthew 9:14–15, enigmatic and paradoxical though they are, are stoked, funded, fueled, and catalyzed by a good idea.

Much of the biblical criticism that I was taught in college and seminary was based upon a methodology whereby the interpreter presumed to divest oneself of all preconceptions and prejudices and interpret the biblical text in free fashion, denuded of all prior conviction.

Obviously nobody can do that. Everyone stands somewhere. We all bring convictions and presuppositions to the biblical text. Even the principle that we ought to interpret free of convictions is itself a conviction.

In this sermon Barth shows the fecundity of approaching the biblical text with a self-evident, unabashed theological point of view. He discovers secrets in the biblical narrative that are unlocked by his theology. So perhaps I am wrong in saying that we preachers don't have enough good ideas driving our sermons. It is perhaps more true to say that we lack a theological point of view that gives us anything of much interest to see in the biblical text and to say in the sermon. Bad theology breeds homiletical boredom.

To say that this sermon is driven by an interesting idea is much too abstract. Energizing this sermon is more than an interesting idea. The person of Christ, colliding with our preconceptions and expectations, drives this sermon. The presence of Christ is not only the subject matter of this sermon but also the agent of the proclamation. As Barth's good friend Bonhoeffer put it:

> The proclaimed word has its origin in the incarnation of Jesus Christ. It neither originates from truth once perceived nor from personal experience. It is not the reproduction of a specific set of feelings. . . . The proclaimed word is the incarnate Christ himself, . . . the thing itself. The preached Christ is both the Historical One and the Present One. . . . The proclaimed word is not a medium of expression for something else, something which lies behind it, but rather is the Christ himself walking through his congregation as the word.[2]

That which makes the Christian faith "more than" merely "religious" is Christ present. That which makes a sermon "more than" a religiously tinted lecture is Jesus walking among his people through the sermon, so that they might throw off their sanctimonious, deadly piety and walk with him.

Many of us preachers base our sermons upon the premise that the thoughts within the sermon are thoughts that the congregation has already had, punctuating our sermons with, "Right?" and "Haven't you always felt that . . . ?" We still preach, all evidence to the contrary, with a Christendom mentality. This culture is at least vestigially Christian. Being Christian is roughly synonymous with being a thinking, caring American. We present the gospel as universally applicable principles and insights that can be utilized by anyone. A sermon contains thoughts that most of us have already thought, yet were unable to express as well as the preacher.

Here is a sermon whose train of thought reminds us that faithful preaching deals with more than commonsense wisdom. The source of a sermon is revelation, the knowledge that comes only from on high, as a gift of God. Barth's sermon is up-front and even exuberant in its apparent supposition that here are thoughts that no one has ever had—before listening to this sermon! Well done, you prophetic troubler of Israel!

January 18, 1920

2 Corinthians 1:3–11

Blessed be the God and Father of our Lord Jesus Christ, the Father of mercies and the God of all consolation, who consoles us in all our affliction, so that we may be able to console those who are in any affliction with the consolation with which we ourselves are consoled by God. For just as the sufferings of Christ are abundant for us, so also our consolation is abundant through Christ. If we are being afflicted, it is for your consolation and salvation; if we are being consoled, it is for your consolation, which you experience when you patiently endure the same sufferings that we are also suffering. Our hope for you is unshaken; for we know that as you share in our sufferings, so also you share in our consolation.

We do not want you to be unaware, brothers and sisters, of the affliction we experienced in Asia; for we were so utterly, unbearably crushed that we despaired of life itself. Indeed, we felt that we had received the sentence of death so that we would rely not on ourselves but on God who raises the dead. He who rescued us from so deadly a peril will continue to rescue us; on him we have set our hope that he will rescue us again, as you also join in helping us by your prayers, so that many will give thanks on our behalf for the blessing granted us through the prayers of many.

1. Last Sunday we spoke about *what the actual situation is* among Paul, and the person of the Bible generally, and us today. We have seen that their secret lies in having *come to themselves*. They have *awakened* out of all kinds of dreams. They no longer wear *masks*. They are *what they are* through the will of God, and they have no wish to be anything else. That is the origin of the brightness that shines around their lives. Why should *we not also* come to ourselves? Why should *we not also* become what we basically are, what we are through the will of God?

2. But entrance into the ranks of the people of the Bible is *not to be had cheaply*. There is good reason that we, in our time more than ever before, sense a distance separating us from them. The time is not entirely gone when Christians rather shamelessly and without hesitation were so bold as to place themselves beside Christ, the prophets, and the apostles and to apply all that is said of them to themselves. We have *also done that*. It is true, is it not? that we sense that it would be a rather bold undertaking if a pastor today compared himself positively to Paul, and if we were to speak of a community of God in Zurich, Basel, or Safenwil, together with all the saints in the canton, as Paul speaks in our text of

the community of God in Corinth and the saints in all Achaia. If we were to speak like that today, we would have to laugh and not believe what we said. *It is good* that we today have gradually become aware of this distance, even if it does have, at first, the consequence that the Bible has become more foreign to us.

In a *presumption of familiarity* we have taken the liberty of tapping the Savior and his disciples on the shoulder, so to speak, as if we were naturally the best of friends, as if being a Christian were something very simple. But this familiarity was only a presumption, and one for which the penalty had to be suffered. For in this way *a kind of Christianity arose* that presumably stood on biblical ground, but lacked the brightness, the earnestness, and the power of life lived by the people of the Bible in each and every area and aspect of their existence. The world has long since seen through the counterfeit as meaningless and turned away from it. It is better for us first to gain *respect again* for these biblical people and to recognize that entry into their ranks is not something easy and self-evident, but bound with very definite conditions and consequences. Jesus himself warned those who wished to follow him: "For which of you, intending to build a tower, does not first sit down and estimate the cost, to see whether he has enough to complete it?" [Luke 14:28].

3. In the text for today we hear that these biblical people are persons who *find themselves in greatest affliction.* They have to carry a *burden* and a yoke, like beasts of burden. They are like *servants* and slaves who have to do heavy work. They are placed on *the watch* alone in dark night. I use expressions from the Bible itself. Here is the basic *difference* between the gospel and that other Christianity as it is presented in the usual Christian books, newspapers, and other such writings, or in the efforts of Christian Science or theosophy. Everywhere we are promised *freedom* from all afflictions and promised happiness, peace of mind, spiritual and physical health, true personal life, even contact with the beyond. The gospel says, "Yes, all that too!" but it goes on to say, "*Beyond all that* you must suffer a very great affliction, and only through this great affliction may you experience freedom from the small afflictions that plague you. You may not *confuse the one with the other*, but you must *see clearly* and *make your choice.*" In contrast, today's kind of Christianity brings us before an *open and accessible heaven* into which a person easily and victoriously steps. The gospel leads us to a *closed door,* and before it we must first remain standing and knocking. Like the authors of those modern books, in which so many today find a replace-

ment for the Bible, the spokespersons of today's religion—including the chapel preachers of the separatist communities in the villages as well as the celebrated pulpit preachers in the cities—give assurance that "those who follow us *will receive what they need easily and beautifully!*" The Bible says: "If any want to become my followers, let them deny themselves and take up their cross and follow me"! [Mark 8:34 par.]. Those two are *not the same.*

4. Paul was certainly *far beyond* most of what afflicts us. What it means to be alone, to have many enemies and few friends, to be misunderstood, to suffer the consequences of one's own mistakes, to drag around a sick body, to be poor and tormented and mistreated, to be in danger of death—he knew all that, and probably better than any of us. But he also knew to give an *answer* to it. Still today we can see in his letters how he was able ever again to ascend over all his suffering. Paul could say to *us modern Christians:* "I know something of what you seek for yourselves, or indeed what you think you have found: happiness, peace within, good character formation, the artful way of dealing with others, deep and beautiful experiences—yes, I am acquainted with all that." He could even say to today's theosophists and spiritists, "I too know something of what is beyond this life!" And to the faith healers: "Healing and being healed through the power of prayer are not foreign to me." But I believe if Paul were alive today, he would not enter into such competition. In any case he did not, although all those things existed then too. He looks beyond all the freedom and successes he undoubtedly had, and *openly confesses,* "I was still in affliction, and I will be again." For now he stands *before the great affliction,* which is not put aside by the real or imagined resolution of other, smaller afflictions by whatever means are available. He confronts the Corinthian community *not as one who has come through affliction*s and can now give them the solution for doing the same, but as one in greater affliction than any of them and who therefore turns to them for help.

5. Paul was in earnest when he spoke of the extent of his affliction, of all his suffering. With us there is always, to some degree at least, *the question* about whether we have the right to sigh about our suffering as earnestly as we often do. If the way *out of affliction is as easy as it appears to be* in religion today, why do we take it so seriously? If today we can *so quickly be calmed,* why did we get so upset yesterday? If *whatever solution* that comes along and appeals to us is right and good, can the evil

we suffer be so great? *Those who really suffer* are more cautious, more reserved, more skeptical, more careful in their choices than we usually are. In order to be able to experience something of real help, perhaps all of us must again learn real suffering.

Paul, in speaking about what he has *suffered,* and not for the first or the last time, says: "We were so utterly, unbearably crushed that we despaired of life itself. . . . We felt we had received the sentence of death!" He feels himself being pushed farther and farther out to the *edge of an abyss.* All comfort, help, and hope *fail.* In the next moment he will stand where no one can stand, where one can only fall and die. All the blossoms and leaves of the tree have *fallen,* and only the sad stump still stands. *Death has won power* over him. Death has become the *only possibility* that he can count on. Yes, death! What is death? Is it the final and perfect savior from the suffering of this life, the proclaimer of the full truth and clarity that we are missing here and now? Yes, perhaps. But perhaps it is only *the riddle* of all riddles, the eternal seal, as it were, on the gruesome message that all existence is meaningless. Death is perhaps really death!

It is no small matter to look death, with its either/or, in the eye. There is good reason for the fact that, when we are in the midst of great difficulties and suffering, we *want rather to avoid* thinking about death. It is good that probably most of those who die do so *without having to think about death. Paul had to think about* death. We do not know what *outer occurrences* led him into this great affliction, whether shipwreck or sickness or persecution. But we do not need to know. *A thousand other persons* have been through experiences just as difficult or more difficult and have not had to think about death—perhaps about dying, yes, but not about death. For them the question, *"What is the whole world,* and what are you, if you must die?" was not urgent and burning. Not for one moment were they in the necessity of contemplating the whole of life *from the standpoint of death.* Not for one moment did they recognize that human life is a task that really does go *far beyond our power,* because we should live and yet cannot because death has power over our life. Not for one moment did everything else—their thoughts, their vocation, their wishes, their faith, their love, their hope, themselves and their fellow human beings, even life itself—become *insignificant, indifferent, and as nothing* over against death and its inexorable question. But all these were true for Paul.

Or has the meaning of death, if only for one moment, become as clear as lightning to us too? Have we ever, even for one moment, seen everything in the lightning-clear clarity of death? *Yes, that can be,* and if so, then we have at least *a sense* of what the question is about. Yet Paul suffered this affliction not just once, but *ever again,* so that this situation—at the outermost edge of being lost, of despair, of nothingness—became *his actual home.* It is true, is it not, that we understand the question "What are all our sufferings *beside this,* and what are the means, great and small, to which we usually resort to meet the distress it causes in us?" Paul's distress is the *great distress* and the great affliction, where everything becomes unsure, where everything is placed in question.

In the *Old Testament* it did not suffice *the prophet Hosea,* who lived with a faithless wife in a most unhappy marriage, to complain about his misfortune and seek some way out of it. Rather, in his personal misfortune as in a picture, he saw the judgment that all Israel and Judah were suffering through their unfaithfulness to God. In an atrocious plague of locusts, the prophet Joel saw not only a dreadful natural event and misfortune of the nation, but also the inbreaking of a great and terrible day of the Lord, from whose power of destruction no help is to be found at all [Joel 2:1–11]. *That is great affliction,* when one realizes what actually lies behind one's small, everyday sufferings; when these small sufferings *grow and grow before one's eyes* until they completely fill all the space between heaven and earth; when darkness makes an end to the last rays of sunlight; *when one realizes one's mortality* and must stare death in the face in the midst of life; when *there is nothing left* but the question, "My God, my God, why have you forsaken me?" [Ps. 22:1; Matt. 27:46 par.].

Paul suffered *this affliction.* He knew what it meant when he said that he must suffer the suffering of Christ. There stand the people of the Bible. They stand *around the cross of Christ,* where all human culture and progress along with all morality and religion are at an end, or rather where they should first begin. Considered from this viewpoint, *the world appears very different.* We do well to take our distance from these biblical people and *carefully consider* whether we wish to step into their ranks.

6. But in this remarkable place where the people of the Bible stand, *something yet more remarkable* happens. Something like the *turn of a great wheel* in the steerage of a great ship, which in happening turns the ship in a different direction. More remarkable than Paul's great affliction are his words: "Blessed be the God and Father of our Lord Jesus Christ, the Father of mercies and the God of all consolation, who consoles us

in all our affliction!" That is *something completely new:* "God," "Father,"
"mercy," "consolation!" How does that come about here, where we
least expect it? For is not *all at its end* when one sees only death before
one, when one can contemplate life only from the standpoint of death?!
It is as if we see a *tired wanderer* climbing higher and higher in the steep
and shadowy crevice of a mountain, on into night and ice. Where will
he go the wrong way, where be lost? All at once he stops; he has come
to *a rim between two valleys.* We see him in the *light of a sun* that does
not shine on us. But it shines on him after he has traversed the entire
area of shadow. We see that he shades his eyes with his hand and looks
afar upon a thousand things that we do not see. But he sees them. He
was not discouraged by the hours of nothing but ice and snow under
his feet and before him; he did not quit the climb. *That is the person of
the Bible. He does not avoid* the thought of death. In his small sufferings he is not content with what is half soothing, half calming, and half
edifying. He goes through the whole affliction, completely through it,
and *then he reaches* a last deepest or highest point, and there the turn
occurs, there the words are "God," "Father," "mercy," "consolation!"
It is true, is it not? that we understand, or at least sense that *there is a
connection* between the great affliction of the person of the Bible and
the real consolation that this person received.

In our small afflictions we do not have this consolation, because
they are *only small* afflictions, because we so anxiously avoid the great,
encompassing affliction, the life- and world-affliction, the affliction of
death. *Happiness* in misfortune, yes, we can have that, and consolation
for a couple of sad days or even years. We can have *experiences* in our life
that is no life, yes, and *a little health* for our sick bodies that still must
die. If we go to the school of the theosophists, we can have even *glimpses
into the beyond.* But God, Father, mercy, consolation, the *Wholly Other*
that does not beautify and cover over death with religion, morality, or
feeling, but annuls death—the Wholly Other that makes us, whether
in life or death, victors over death—this we do not have in our small
afflictions. And this is the reason why, even though they are only small
afflictions, they are so very heavy. They are heavy because they are not
yet heavy in the last extreme. We have to sigh so much because we have
not yet *rightly* learned to sigh. We have to pass away and die because we
do not know death and do not want to know it.

God, Father, mercy, consolation: these are *beyond the mountain,*
beyond the great affliction, not this side of it. "*Flesh and blood* cannot
inherit the Kingdom of God" [1 Cor. 15:50]. *We must pass away* before

we can be. We must be born anew before we can live [cf. John 3:3]. *"This perishable body must put on* imperishability, and this mortal body must put on immortality" [1 Cor. 15:53]. *Time must be fulfilled* by eternity. That is the necessary *turn and transformation* given by God. That is the *resurrection,* the only real answer to the question that all of us, even today, carry in our hearts. *God is not* one of the many idols that we erect to make life tolerable in this world of death, but the God who wakes the dead, "who calls into existence things that do not exist" [Rom. 4:17]. The people of the Bible make their way *to this God;* they do not pass the great affliction by, but go through it. And as they go through it, they also understand why it had to be: so that we do not set our trust in ourselves, but in the God who wakes the dead. *Of this God* the people of the Bible can then boast: God has saved us and will save us from this death; in God we hope for continuing salvation. The people of the Bible *live* because they are mortal, because they do not refuse to die daily and hourly to that to which one must die [cf. 1 Cor. 15:31]. We do understand, do we not? the words, *"Blessed are those who mourn,* for they will be comforted" [Matt. 5:4].

One could also say, "Blessed are those who put *their trust* no longer in themselves, for they will experience God's grace!" Or, "Blessed are those who *know no answer,* for they will receive the answer." Tolstoy described this in his story *The Death of Ivan Ilych.* He tells how a healthy person *becomes ill* and slowly must take his leave of life, although he does not want to leave it and constantly asks God and other persons for health, relief, comfort, for thoughts other than thoughts of death. But he finds less and less of these wherever he asks. On his deathbed he still resists death, still wishes to return to health. Finally he feels himself as if thrust into a narrow, dark, long *enclosure,* and still he resists until he finally yields. At the end of this enclosure *a small light* appears. He sees it, rejoices, and dies. Look, *that is where the person of the Bible begins:* where human being yields. Yet this is not yielding to death, but yielding to the passage through death.

It is here that the life of *the most consoled and comforted person* begins. For the small, distant light that falls from the other side into our life in the here and now—*that is the consolation,* the real comfort. When we yield to the passage through death, our suffering becomes a *suffering with the suffering of Christ.* And then, as the suffering of Christ comes richly over us, we are richly comforted through Christ. *Yes, richly.* Whoever even once sees this little light, even if only from afar, knows that it is truly consolation enough. It does not have to be a light to us *for the first time* at the hour of death; not then do we need to become biblical persons for the first time. *For Paul it was light in his life* in the here and now. *His life* was lived in the light of the resurrection.

There he stands, and stands ever again, before the *great affliction.* We might rather want to *pity* him and *guard* ourselves against going through that passage. We might want to run away with our small burdens to get rid of them somewhere else. But he—he goes into and through it, *turns the wheel of steerage,* and the great, heavy ship obeys, and all at once it becomes clear *who God is and where God stands.* The light of the resurrection shines, and a strong, brave man, a man who is sure and certain, steps courageously into time and the world. The power of the beyond has become *the power of the here and now. Life* has come out of death. *What should one fear* who has no fear of death? How should one *fear dying* who has known death and found life in death? Hear his jubilation: "Blessed be the God and Father of our Lord Jesus Christ, the Father of mercy and the God of all consolation, who consoles us in all our affliction!"

7. We want to discuss this text again next Sunday, for there is still more in it. But it is true, is it not? that we see something of *the people of the Bible,* the people of God. We see how *distant* we are from them and yet *how much we need* to be near them. We *too* would like to be *the people of God.* We are tired of digging out "cracked cisterns" of water and of "sowing among thorns" [Jer. 2:13; 4:3]. Why should we too not become the people of God in suffering and in glory? When we read such words as those of our text and contemplate them respectfully from a distance, we cannot possibly do so without sensing that we are not excluded, but *included, invited* to go with them. And perhaps there is something in us today that is already *going with them.*

COMMENTS

Don't you find it curious that Barth—who had so vivid a sense of God's active presence—continues through this period to stress God's absence? In an ironic sense, it is as if the closer to God, the true and living God, that Barth was drawn through his study of Paul's Letters, the more Barth realized that here was a God who is not easily enlisted into our religious projects, is not the God who was vaguely presented to him as a seminarian, the God who is not accessible through our means of making sense of the world, a God who is at some remove even from the church that thinks its mission is to come close to God. In October 1920 Barth began a fevered rewrite of *Romans*, determined to say even more explicitly what he had said in the previous edition, eager utterly to purge his thought of any vestiges of his old, liberal elements. God isn't humanity uttered in a loud voice.

Is that not one of the major reasons why we preachers preach—to lessen the gap between us and God? In this sermon, Barth tries to widen the gap. It is as if Barth claims that nearness with God begins with respect for the distance between us and God and that for us to think that we have at last succeeded in becoming tight with God is to prove how badly we have misunderstood God. So Barth warns his congregation of a "closed door," of the "threat," of "conditions" that God places between us and God, mocking our vaunted claims of being able to approach God through our thoughts and our experience. Calling upon the prophets Hosea and Joel to stand with Paul as witnesses, Barth proclaims a dead end for all our "culture and progress along with all morality and religion."

Once again, an attack upon religion—defined in *Romans* as "a vigorous and extensive attempt to humanize the divine, . . . to make it a practical 'something,' for the benefit of those who cannot live with the Living God, and yet cannot live without God."[1] Some of Barth's anti-religion polemic is attributable to Luther's stress upon justification as solely the work of God, not our works, including the work that is called "church." I expect that a major source for Barth's attack was his more extensive encounter, during 1919, with the thought of Kierkegaard, the melancholy Dane who so sharply drew the line between "Christendom" in Denmark and following Jesus Christ. "Religion" consists of all the ways we humans try to climb up to the God who cannot be approached, but only received. But I also wonder if Barth sours on "religion" because as a pastor at Safenwil he is now in the thick of its most debilitating effects. It would take a pastor, bogged down in the numbing routine of daily life in the church, to know that, whatever the gospel is, it is other than, or considerably more than, our "religion."

Thus Barth in this sermon cites the "wholly other" of Rudolf Otto, whose 1917 book on "The Holy" (*Das Heilige*) was all the rage. God is that One of whom nothing higher can be thought or said. Furthermore, if we serve the God of the Bible, we serve a God who resurrects. Only the dead get raised from the dead, so in order to be with a living God, we must die to our illusory attempts to get to God and must mortify our vaunted intellect, allowing God to raise, in God's own way, us good-as-dead people. God can only be received as God is, not as we desire.

Isn't this odd talk for a preacher? A preacher has the business of speaking to people close to God, not announcing the unbridgeable distance from God. Here is a sermonic embodiment of Barth's contention, as a preacher, that preaching is impossible. Is this a self-destructive theology? In a sense, yes. Barth proclaims a religion that is antireligion, talk about God that is deeply suspicious of all talk about God, a nearness to God that results in a great sense of God's utter distance from us. One reason why we crucified Jesus was because Jesus was not the God whom we expected or even wanted. So much for our "religion."

Here Barth is moving along the *via negativa*. We best speak of God by saying what we know that God is not. The only way to God is no way, or at least not the way that is our way. Only God can speak of God. Theology cannot be our words about God; it must be God's Word to us. This is bracing, invigorating stuff, refreshing to hear from a preacher who is supposed to know so very much about God.

And yet one cannot always walk a way that is no way. To say what God is not is to imply that one knows who God truly is. The negative "We can say nothing truthful about God" tends also to negate the very statement "We can say nothing." Homiletic irony becomes a self-consuming practice. One can't preach God as "wholly other" every Sunday. Eventually a preacher must come forward and say that, while we don't know God, God has made God's self known in Jesus Christ, confronting our smug irony with the fact of a Jew from Nazareth who is God. The recognition that God has indeed definitively spoken in Jesus Christ and that the Trinity continues to speak now was one of the major moves Barth made post-Safenwil in his *Church Dogmatics.*

Perhaps saying what God is not is a necessary first step toward a solid notion of who God is. The *via negativa* eventually led Barth to surer footing. In this sermon, Barth speaks forthrightly, if not too specifically, of the strange "conditions" that Christ puts upon us. Perhaps Barth is implying that God seems so unapproachable and strange in great part because we have made erroneous assumptions of God, demanding who God should be if we are to worship this God. In an odd way publicly to admit that one does not know the true and living God is ironically to show that one is coming close, much nearer to the true and living God. Thus Barth's sermons are full of irony: here is one speaking about that which cannot be spoken. And here is a preacher telling the church that it is not really the body of Christ, even though there is no way for the preacher to know that they are not the body of Christ except through the tools given to the preacher (1 Corinthians) from the body of Christ.

We contemporary preachers seem flummoxed between the (liberal) dilemma of a "false modesty" (John Milbank) that denies knowing anything when it comes to God talk, or a kind of (conservative evangelical) arrogant posture of too-easy assertions about exactly who God is and what God demands. Both theological liberals and conservatives fail to appreciate the deeply ironical nature of preaching. Barth framed our challenge: We cannot speak about God; we are under compulsion as preachers to speak about God. Irony is bracing, invigorating, and sounds insightful and intelligent. Any preacher who boldly admits what human words and human thoughts and deeds cannot do with God has good biblical ground upon which to stand. And yet, irony has a debilitating quality. Eventually the preacher must speak, must make a claim upon the hearers, must admit to standing somewhere, must think through the implications of sermonic assertions, must testify to a God who, though we had nothing much to say to God, spoke to us, became Word incarnate, unavoidable, concrete, specific, too close to home for comfort.

One year after Barth preached this sermon, he would be invited to be a professor at Göttingen. The lecture hall would force Barth to say more, and to say it more assertively and systematically than he had in the pulpit. I confess to some regret as I watch Barth put much of his youthful irony behind him and move on to more concrete, intellectually coherent, systematically biblical assertions of the presence and claims of God-with-us. Fortunately he moved to academia not before preaching some wonderfully honest, engaging sermons in Safenwil, such as this one in January of 1920.

February 29, 1920

2 Corinthians 2:5–11

If anyone has caused pain, he has caused it not to me, but to some extent—not to exaggerate it—to all of you. This punishment by the majority is enough for such a person; so now instead you should forgive and console him, so that he may not be overwhelmed by excessive sorrow. So I urge you to reaffirm your love for him. I wrote for this reason: to test you and to know whether you are obedient in everything. Anyone whom you forgive, I also forgive. What I have forgiven, if I have forgiven anything, has been for your sake in the presence of Christ. And we do this so that we may not be outwitted by Satan; for we are not ignorant of his designs.

The way of the grace of God, which we must find and then take, is a mountain path leading high above, between two abysses. It is not an easy path and does not provide us with a nice walk. One can find a nice walk only on one of the two roads that lead left and right in the valley below, but on these roads we remain in the valley and do not achieve the goal. On the high mountain path we also cannot step just anywhere. In every moment there is only *one* right possibility, one right place to put one's foot. All other possibilities are in truth not possibilities at all, for they end in a fall into the depths. Stepping in the right place becomes all the more difficult the higher we climb. We also cannot rest and make ourselves comfortable, for there is simply no place for a rest, and no moment of our life is suited to it. Like Elijah on the way to the mountain called Horeb, we have a great distance before us and cannot afford to make camp; but after we have received the strength of the heavenly food, we must continue for forty days and forty nights [1 Kgs. 19:8]. We have no choice but to keep moving forward on this way attentively, carefully and without stopping. Something of this moving forward is also described in our text.

A member of the community of Christians in Corinth has insulted Paul. We do not know what it was about, but it must have severely wronged him. What would we do in such a situation? Look there, the two abysses to the right and the left. The abyss on the left would say, "I cannot overcome it; I am deeply wounded. This person is from now on a black mark in my life, and in all I think, say, and do, it will be more or less obvious that he has done me wrong and that I will have nothing more to do with him." If we put our foot there or stop to rest, we will fall into an abyss. For whether that person had no reason at all to wrong me, or whether the wrong he did me was in part an answer to a wrong that was in me, whichever was the case, something in me—and indeed the best in me, my immortal soul—remains untouched by such an experience and cannot be deeply wounded. We are all something other than the self that can be wounded and hurt by such an experience.

For this reason I perhaps can, in recognition of the wrong in me, let the experience cause me to repent. It is also possible that I have to defend myself. But I cannot place myself in the terrible cage of a deadly insult and simply stare helplessly at the wrong that was done me, as a trapped bird stares at the snake that is about to eat it. If I did that, I would betray my soul and fall from grace. That was Paul's thought. He shook off the wrong. "This person has not caused me pain," he says. He will not allow a black, empty mark to arise within him; he will remain free. That is the way of grace.

To the right is another abyss. There one would say, "It does not bother me that such a person says something about me; I have thick skin, and I can despise and forget him." Perhaps we have wished we could deal with an injury in that way. Perhaps we have received such good advice from our friends and acquaintances: "You must ignore it, do not think about it; let them say what they will; what does it matter to you?" But it is so difficult to follow this advice that we may soon realize it that cannot be good advice. Saying "it does not matter to me" is never great wisdom, for the human heart is warm and not cold. When we experience evil, we cannot take it lightly or make it insignificant. That would be but another abyss, or another cage in which we trap ourselves. When the passion that fights in us against evil is extinguished, we are dead, although the body continues to live. When we can no longer be angry, we have lost our soul.

Paul can say, "He has not caused me pain!" but he does not make the sin against him into something insignificant; he rather sees it as very significant, and he continues, "He has caused all of you pain." He does not let himself be bound by the evil that has happened to him, but he is both sad and angry about the hindrance that has once again been put in the way of the working of God among human beings. Insofar as the experience strikes against his person, his self, it is for Paul unimportant. What is important is the disruption of Spirit, community, and hope that is now cast like a shadow over him and the Christians in Corinth. That is why he apparently dealt with this person energetically and with severity in the earlier letter he had written. He is not full of personal bitterness, but he is angry. He does not feel personally insulted, but he is indignant. He has no interest in personal conflict, but he does fight the evil. He has shaken off the injustice done him, but only in order to pick it up and carry it.—Do you now see the path that leads high above between the two abysses?

In the meanwhile in Corinth something has apparently been done to correct this person. As a healthy body defends itself against an invading virus, so the people of Corinth have given this person to understand that by his words against Paul, he has broken community with them and disturbed the Spirit they had with one another. They understood that it was not a matter of a personal insult, but an attack against the message of Jesus, something that concerned them all. That is also a sign of the vitality of early Christianity: the way personal matters are illumined by a light that transcends the merely personal. For them personal matters were not so important as they are for us, and yet they took them much more seriously than we do. If someone had wandered into the desert and gotten lost, like this person, he immediately recognized that he was in the desert. There was no misunderstanding and no covering up; they spoke openly, directly, and imposed punishment, often quickly and with fearsome effect. They could act in this way and they had to act in this way, for there was something new and holy in their midst, something that itself resisted what threatened it. And for this reason Paul could now write that it was enough, the punishment had accomplished its purpose, so there was no need to continue it.

We too are used to punishing one another, although in doing so we are certainly very arbitrary. We cover up for one another most things and usually precisely the worst, but when it suits us, we can be harsh, sending whoever is concerned into the desert. That is another difference from those first Christians: on such occasions we hit hard and know no limit. We have no purpose in mind for the punishment, and so also we are not thinking about its limits. What rather happens is that we blindly go on with malicious words and faces, spite, exclusion, and finally indifference, so that the person feels enclosed in a coldness like that at the North Pole. There are people with faults that endure years and perhaps a lifetime of punishment, and usually these are not the worst persons we know. So we swing arbitrarily to and fro between overlooking and covering up on the one hand, and blind rage on the other. Our inflicting of punishment arises not out of life but death. It is not what is holy and therefore new in us that defends itself, but our confusion, which causes us to strike out because we do not know what to do against the evil that offends us.

Punishment must have a purpose, even if it is only an angry look. Scholars and scientists argue about whether the purpose of punishment is to improve a person or to protect society from the person. The first Christians had no need to argue about this. For them the opposition between society and individual did not exist because every individual was a member of a body, and this indivisible whole had the purpose of honoring Christ as its head [cf. Col. 1:18]. If punishment had to be, it came about because the honor of Christ had been abused, and it had no other purpose than to restore this honor. It may be difficult for us to translate these thoughts of the first Christians into our own because our life is not the life from which these thoughts arose. But given the high purpose that it had for those first Christians, we do intuit that the punishment could not have been hard, wooden, and without limit. It could have a powerfully shaking effect, but it also ended, and indeed for the same reason that it had been imposed.

Why did Paul say that the punishment should end? Because the one who insulted him should not be consumed by the affliction of the punishment. Paul does not say it out of pity or lenience, but on the contrary out of the greatest zeal for God. And this zeal now brings relief to the one punished. It is thought and spoken from God and Christ, when Paul, after having called for severity, now asks his friends to cease with severity and to forgive and console. In the entire Bible we see that the people of the Bible were not inclined to "all too much" of anything: all too much godlessness, all too much righteousness, all too much power, all too much joy, and all too much affliction—all that should not be. Everything that is all too much consumes human beings, for it makes them unfit for God and God's work; it erects a wall between them and God's will, salvation, and forgiveness. The people of God should stand and walk, but not all too securely. If necessary they must be broken, for which, depending on the circumstances, punishment may serve as the means, but again not all too much, for they should not be destroyed. "The bruised reed he will not break" [Isa. 42:3; cf. German]. It is important that an element of courage remain in the person. And so Paul says, as it were, "No arrogance when you punish, and no destruction!" That is why, after the punishment, he calls for love and forgiveness. In this case the arrogance was perhaps on the side of his friends, who with their zeal sent their enemy into the desert and wanted to leave him there. They should not become Pharisees, for if they did, in the midst of their good work Satan would have won the game. On the other hand, if they had continued to punish without ceasing, then destruction, bitterness, and despair would have been the fate of the enemy, and this again would have been the triumph of the devil. For the sake of God, neither may happen. In God all must remain connected, enemies and friends, and therefore also punishment and forgiveness. Would that not be a great experience of salvation for us and for those who are evil, if we could again come into this connection, if we could again learn to fear God and hence to avoid the "all too much"?

Therefore Paul admonishes the Corinthians to love the person who has given offense. That is remarkable, and it is meaningful only on the way of grace and of God and only so to be understood. In this admonition to love, we see how seriously Paul meant that the punishment was only one side of forgiveness, and for this reason it should not go too far. It can happen that we forgive someone but dislike seeing that others forgive and accept him. We have contained our anger but would like to see the anger work a littler further through others. Perhaps it would be a test of whether our punishing and forgiveness are genuine and true, whether they have their origin in grace and God, if we could say to others, "I myself, who have been insulted, admonish you again to love the one who has insulted me." We would not have to say it only with words.

Something else that is notable in what Paul says is the fact that he can presuppose that the readers of his letter have love and only need to let love rule, as one might open a faucet and the water simply and self-evidently flows. Among the first Christians was a love that was always there, that never ceased, as Paul elsewhere writes [1 Cor. 13:8], a love that was ready and waiting during the punishment, a love also within hating, despising, and rejecting, which only needed to take off this foreign clothing in order to show itself again as wholly and completely love. It was a power that the Christians in all cases possessed and that they only had to use. It is true, is it not? that all of this is so strong, so simple, so helpful! May God give us a new access to this self-evidently ruling love.

Paul writes in our text, "I wrote for this reason: to test you and to know whether you are obedient in everything." This too is rightly said out of the heart of the Bible. He had written them earlier that they should punish the one who had insulted him. But if they rightly understood him, they also recognized that it was for Paul not so much a matter of the punishment itself, but of their obedience, of the insight, goodwill, and Christian character of their actions. He did not simply command, "There must be punishment!" No, there was to be punishment only as a piece, only as a moment, of a whole Christian movement. In another moment something else had to take its place, and indeed the opposite of what was done before! It was an occasion for obedience—not obedience to Paul naturally, but in all things obedience to the voice of God, a voice that is always new: this obedience was what he wanted from them. Now there is another occasion for obedience. If they learned something yesterday, they will prove it today. That is the ability for movement of the people of the Bible, which is something we cannot see clearly enough. Because of their flexibility and their energetic freedom for movement, the people of the Bible never become rigid, never rust away, never decay like dead fruit, but "mount up with wings like eagles" [Isa. 40:31].

The final words of the text draw together all that Paul has said here: "What I have forgiven, if I have forgiven anything, has been for your sake in the presence of Christ. And we do this so that we may not be outwitted by Satan; for we are not ignorant of his designs." What is the secret of this whole text? It is one of many texts in the Bible, and one of many in 2 Corinthians, that we usually pass by without much attention. What is its secret? I believe its secret lies in the words, "for your sake in the presence of Christ." We see Paul standing like a soldier before his king, a soldier who has no other interest than doing his work correctly in the eyes of the king. He may not do it poorly; he must be circumspect and careful, because the king is watching. This circumspection and carefulness prompt Paul to forgive "for your sake," for the sake of the host of those among whom Christ will dwell on earth, until he can reveal himself. He does it "for your sake," so that among them no bitterness, no offense, and no halting of movement occur. What he personally has to forgive plays no role in this. He does not forgive because he is so full of goodness and understanding or because he is of noble character, but "for your sake in the presence of Christ."

We must ever again return to these words if we want to understand Paul and the way of grace that he travels as the sinful, imperfect person he was. The grace that Paul knows is the only grace there is: It makes one insensitive to wrongs done to one's person; it makes one avid, rigorous, and understanding; it makes one watchful of the proud and merciful to those who have been humbled. It gives the love that bears all things, hopes all things, and endures all things [1 Cor. 13:7]. It gives the wisdom to require nothing of persons by requiring everything from them. Today we live in a time when everything threatens to fall apart because human beings cannot forgive one another, and this quite apart from whether they are, in human terms, in the right or in the wrong. We live in a time when things threaten to fall apart, because the cleverness of Satan is so very successful in hardening human beings toward one another. And indeed perhaps everything must fall apart, because the only connection that can hold it together has been so completely lost and must now be sought anew. May there be persons here and there who find the way to one another; who quietly lay a new ground for life in the world; who desire the way of grace and will risk going this way, never to leave it—and who perhaps have already found it.

COMMENTS

Stanley Hauerwas says that when Methodists say "grace," we have no idea what we're talking about. This sermon goes a long way in explaining why "grace" is so inexplicable. "Grace" is the impact of a living God upon the world. God's free grace will not be domesticated by us. Grace is "a mountain path leading high above, between two abysses." This is a marvelous opening metaphor that warns us of the perilous theological path that lies before anyone who dares to speak of "grace." (I wish the preacher had stuck with the mountain-path metaphor throughout the sermon, but Barth abandons it, soon after a strong beginning, only to recall it briefly at the end.)

"A member of the community has insulted Paul." With this the preacher deftly contextualizes his sermon and frames the discussion of grace in the concrete communal setting of the need for forgiveness. There are missteps to the left and to the right along this perilous path of grace-induced forgiveness—permissive nonchalance on the one hand and vengeful retribution on the other. Barth praises the church at Corinth for confronting and correcting the one who insulted Paul. For the church to make a communal concern of something that we tend to relegate to the realm of a personal and private grievance is "a sign of the vitality of early Christianity."

Alas, our way of confronting wrong is "very arbitrary" because we have all but lost the theological, ecclesial purpose of punishment for wrongdoing. Paul, says Barth, was motivated neither by leniency nor spite; instead, Paul acted "out of the greatest zeal for God." This is the context for Paul's exhortation to the Corinthians not only to limit the punishment but also to "love" the malefactor. All of this practice of grace, this forgiveness and love, is "in the presence of Christ." No humanitarian impulse and no positive assessment of human nature motivates Paul. Rather, ethics is here a form of worship, behavior that arises from a vivid sense of divine presence. "The King is watching." Recipients of divine grace are gracious toward others, particularly those who are fellow Christian strugglers and attempt to live in the community that is created and sustained by divine grace.

The sermon ends in a poignant plea. "Today we live in a time when everything threatens to fall apart because human beings cannot forgive one another." This is the devil's work. The preacher pleads for people who "find the way to one another" by risking the narrow way of Christ. That narrow way of graciousness to one another is but a retracing of the steps that God in Christ has made to each of us, malefactors all.

A few months before he preached this sermon, Barth gave his famous lecture to a group of fellow pastors at Tambach. That lecture signified some dramatic shifts in Barth's thought about politics. For many weeks in early 1919, Barth was preoccupied with the great general strike. Like any good socialist sympathizer, Barth had given much support to the striking workers. His support for the strike had cost him a good deal of support from the few wealthy members of his congregation.

In the Tambach lecture Barth announced a different and even more radical approach to Christian involvement in politics. He urged, not a quietistic retreat, but a deeper political engagement, an engagement that arises out of the gospel's peculiar assertions about what is really going on in the history of the world. Most of what we call "politics," said Barth, is a trivial sideshow unworthy of the majestic witness of the church. The revolution of God in Jesus Christ, God's devastating, re-creating move upon the world, that is the real revolution. We don't change the world or build a better world through political action; God is doing that. The most politically relevant thing we can do is to preach, to sign, to signal, and to witness to the new world that God is creating in Jesus Christ. This is the heart of Barthian "politics," and it is clearly the background for this sermon's comments about the peculiar, radically odd way that Christians can help the world. In today's church, where preaching in a "prophetic" or "socially relevant" way too often means siding with the secular political right or left, Barth's vision of peculiarly Christian "politics" is still refreshing.

I found this sermon to be most satisfying. It is as if by 1920 Barth has found his voice, asserting with greater clarity and simplicity what

God has given him to say, allowing his expressive, metaphorical tendencies greater play in the sermon, permitting the biblical text to drive the thought and form of the sermon. In reading through Barth's early sermons, one of my discoveries is that 2 Corinthians plays an even larger part in Barth's sermons after 1918 than does Romans. In 2 Corinthians, Paul's constant stresses on the theology of the cross, on power in weakness, on the source of apostolic authority, and on the frustrations of ministry seem to resonate with Barth the often-frustrated pastor. "For we are not peddlers of God's word like so many; but in Christ we speak as persons of sincerity, as persons sent from God" (2 Cor. 2:17). Barth's lifelong stress on the preacher as one "sent from God," whose sermons can be heard only as they are "from God" (*ek theou*), has its roots in this period, in which he learned, like Paul, to rely not on his own rhetorical strengths but rather on the power of God.[1]

This is also one of the most self-evidently pastoral of Barth's early sermons, showing a real concern to speak as a pastor to a concrete, specific Christian community that struggles with the embodiment of the gospel. This sermon therefore is a fine sermonic embodiment of the intent of Paul's pastoral letter itself. The sermon does much of what the text tries to do. Communal concerns were surely Paul's major intent in writing to the Corinthians. As contemporary preachers, we must therefore allow Paul (and Barth) to purge us of two distinctly unbiblical tendencies found at large among us preachers: (1) the tendency to speak to individuals and (2) the inclination to generalize and universalize. When Paul says "you," he almost never means the second-person singular. Paul writes letters addressed to specific congregations, not to isolated individuals. The idea that the gospel is a message addressed to individual hearts and minds is not that of Paul.

Furthermore, Paul's interests tend to be almost exclusively parochial and ecclesial, corporate and communal. His goal was therefore to provoke congregational embodiment of the gospel more than to win general intellectual assent to the gospel. We North American preachers made a big mistake when we began presenting the Christian faith as if it were a set of ideas and principles of relevance to the general populace rather than as the peculiar communal response of those whose world has been undone and redone by being "in the presence of Christ." Our thin ecclesiology leads us to offer the gospel as if it is a word addressed to all thinking, sensitive North Americans rather than as a judgment upon and edification for the church.

April 4, 1920

1 Corinthians 15:50–58

What I am saying, brothers and sisters, is this: flesh and blood cannot inherit the kingdom of God, nor does the perishable inherit the imperishable. Listen, I will tell you a mystery! We will not all die, but we will all be changed, in a moment, in the twinkling of an eye, at the last trumpet. For the trumpet will sound, and the dead will be raised imperishable, and we will be changed. For this perishable body must put on imperishability, and this mortal body must put on immortality. When this perishable body puts on imperishability, and this mortal body puts on immortality, then the saying that is written will be fulfilled: "Death has been swallowed up in victory. Where, O death, is your victory? Where, O death, is your sting?" The sting of death is sin, and the power of sin is the law. But thanks be to God, who gives us the victory through our Lord Jesus Christ.

Therefore, my beloved, be steadfast, immovable, always excelling in the work of the Lord, because you know that in the Lord your labor is not in vain.

1. Do we want to risk coming close to the *enigma of Easter*? But can we not come close? For this enigma is also the entire *content of the Bible*. It has no other content than this: Easter, resurrection, out of death into life! If this were not the Bible's content, we could close it and lay it aside forever. If the Bible does not tell us this, it tells us nothing. And what it tells us is the whole *truth of Christianity*. Beside this truth, there is no room for any other. If Christianity did not carry this truth within it, it would have long since disappeared because of its weakness and lack of honesty. And that truth is also the *meaning of our whole existence*. We live from it, even when we do not know we live from it. If this were not the meaning of our whole existence, how would we be able to exist? For it holds us. Otherwise nothing holds us. There are so many here today who do not often attend church. How should I say to them anything other than the one thing in which all else is contained, the revelation that is full of mystery, and the mystery that is full of revelation? Christ is risen; he is truly risen! [cf. Luke 24:34].

And it is true, is it not? that you all wish to hear me say nothing other than this. You want me not to pass it by, but to go into it and speak out of it; and you know as well as I that the resurrection of Christ is what Easter is about. *Perhaps I cannot* say it simply or clearly or strongly enough—not with the proof of the Spirit and of power [cf. 1 Cor. 2:4] that it would have to be said—but I do want at least to have said it. *Perhaps you cannot* completely understand it, or be completely agreed, or cannot completely go along with this Easter message, but who can completely go along with it? I, at least, cannot! But you should at least have heard what you really do want to hear. We *all go* about as far as we can when we look at Easter from afar and see it, so to speak, like a high alpine mountain whose snowy peaks are veiled in clouds and mist. But we want at least to turn in the direction of the Alps and take note of this mountain, even if we do not see it well. Let us say, "There, there it is, the mystery of revelation; there we would have to seek and ask further; there we would have further to think and pray about it; there great vistas would have to open to us."

2. What is Easter? Easter is Jesus as he is, Jesus as victor. Paul describes it in our text: "Thanks be to God, who gives us the victory through our Lord Jesus Christ." It is not enlightenment, nor a model to imitate, nor a religion, nor a church that gives us the victory. It is Jesus.

He places us human beings *before the final questions* of our existence: "Who are you, where do you come from, where are you going?" We are still *asleep* as long as these final questions are forgotten, circumvented, or suppressed—as long as the questions are silent. But in Jesus we *awaken.* For in Jesus the questions speak; in him they stand before us clearly, unequivocally, and unavoidably. He does not throw these questions up as would a prophet, or as would a philosopher, or a poet, or a preacher. Rather, he throws them up by answering them. Humanity belongs to God. God is the beginning and the end. It is God who "effects both the will and the work" [cf. Phil. 2:13]. He gives this answer not as teaching or opinion, but as *fact.* He proves all of it by doing it: He is obedient to God "to the point of death, even death on the cross" [Phil. 2:8, German]. He is victor. That is Easter.

Jesus stirs up the last doubt in us. This doubt is not simply doubt about our foolish thoughts and the bad things we do; nor doubt about whether our insights and the good that we do really are right; nor doubt about all that is great, important, and holy; nor doubt about the state or the church or the school. Rather, this doubt asks, "What is true? What is good? What is really valuable?" We are still *sleeping* as long as this last doubt is silent. In Jesus we *awaken,* for in Jesus the doubts speak louder, more powerfully, and in a way that overturns everything more than in all the criticisms of the world. For his doubt does not come from a "No," but from a "*Yes*"; it comes from *love,* from the *certainty* that *God* is true and good, and God alone. Can what human beings themselves call true and good stand before God? And what do we need other than God, since all truth and goodness is in God? See how *these things break through together* to us in Jesus: doubt and certainty, no and yes. But what is superior is the certainty, the triumphant "Yes!" Rome and Jerusalem are conquered in him, as is all Jewish and heathen pride, and all Christian pride is conquered before it happens. As for human truth and goodness, when they accomplish as much as they possibly can, they get no further than the crucifixion of the Son of God. But he says, "Father, forgive them. . . . into your hands I commend my spirit" [Luke 23:34, 46]. Jesus is victor! That is Easter.

Jesus places us in *a final insecurity,* not only in our relationship to ourselves and other people, but also in our relationship to the world and all that is. What is the world? What is nature? history? fate? What is the space in which we exist, and what is the time in which we live? What do we really know? What does it mean that we know only what we are able to know? As long as this final insecurity is not disclosed in us, we are still *sleeping.* But in Jesus *we awaken.* The insecurity is disclosed. The sure ground of our understanding begins to quake and sway beneath our feet. We may relate to Jesus as we wish, but this is completely clear: Jesus counts on *God,* and that means on an existence, a being, a power that is in no place and at no time. He stands in the service of a *power* that breaks through fate. He knows a *history,* and he himself is the hero of this history, but it is not world history. There flashes like lightning in him a nature that is on the verge of blowing away what we call nature, as dynamite blows away rock. He lives in a *world* that is not our world. "Heaven and earth will *pass away*!" [Mark 13:31 par.]. And even if the whole New Testament were a fable, this fable would have the highly remarkable meaning that in it *a certainty* emerges that makes everything else uncertain. "I saw a *new* heaven and a new earth" [Rev. 21:1]. That is Jesus. He is victor. And that is Easter.

Jesus leads us *to the final boundary* of our existence. It is the boundary we know so well, and yet do not know: the boundary of death. As long as we do not well consider that we must die, we will *not gain wisdom* [cf. Ps. 90:12]. In Jesus *we gain wisdom,* because, whether we like it or not, the wisdom of Jesus is *the wisdom of death,* as an insightful thinker of our time has said [Franz Overbeck].

Remembering death lies both as the great shadow as well as the great light on all the ways of Jesus. *The Son of Man must suffer,* and he must die [cf. Mark 8:31 par.]. That is the divine compulsion and the divine freedom in Jesus. God begins *where human being ends.* The truth is *beyond the grave.* Out of *death* into life!

But in this wisdom of death there is no renunciation, no sad resignation, nothing at all of melancholy and being sorry for oneself. Out of death into *life:* this is what is meant. For this reason the boundary and limit of human beings should come to consciousness, so that one knows *who God is,* both as the Creator and as the Redeemer. Obedience to the point of death has to be, so that death too may come *under the lordship of God. The same hand* that is nailed to the cross is also the hand that blesses the sick and breaks the bonds of death in which they suffer. *The same mouth* that speaks of having to die also says, "I am the resurrection and the life" [John 11:25]. *The same body* that is killed on Good Friday cannot be found in the grave at Easter [Mark 16:6 par.].

The boundary is reached in order to be *crossed.* To go into death with God means that life goes into death and life comes *out of* death. "Where, O death, is your victory? Where, O death, is your sting?" Let anyone who can understand this, understand it; and "let anyone with ears to hear listen!" [Mark 4:9 par.]. The boundary, the final boundary, is reached in order to be *crossed.* Jesus is victor! That is Easter.

Easter is *the last, behind which stands the first.* One could also say: Easter is the last, out of which the divine first breaks through like the sun breaks through the clouds; or like the stalk grows from the grain of wheat that lies dying in the earth [cf. John 12:24]; or like the child is born from the womb of the suffering mother; or like our thoughts spring from the variegated mass of what we see and experience. But those are only analogies. *Jesus, as he is,* is the reality that analogies can only reflect. A final *restless disquiet,* from which the first real rest and peace emerge; *a final question,* in which the first real answer lies; a final *shudder,* from which for the first time there can in all seriousness be real meaning in the words, "Peace be with you!" [Luke 24:36 par.] A final deep, from which something all at once ascends to the highest! That is Jesus as he is.

Paul says that with the *sound of the last trumpet* the dead will rise imperishable and the rest of us will be changed. The last and yet the first: the decisive, effective, creative *Word of God*—that is Easter. That *this Word has been spoken:* this is what we must say and hear today. We have no intention of dealing with the question about how much we do or do not *believe.* At Easter the disciples of Jesus were much divided in themselves between belief and unbelief. How should we not be? What is most important is that this Word of God has been spoken. And *in us all* there is, more than ever, a question, a doubt, an uncertainty, and an awareness of death. Who is free of it? It may seem that it is the darkest thing in us, and yet it could be the brightest and what is actually living in us. It could also be that we are *waking up* because the sound of the last trumpet has *reached* us. It is possible that, just as we are here today, we could become witnesses to one another that the all-deciding Word of God, the Word of the resurrection, has been *spoken*. How should we be nearer to unfaith than to faith?

3. Let me make several remarks about our text. A man who himself had many insights once called this text, this fifteenth chapter of 1 Corinthians, "an ocean of insights" [Friedrich Oetinger]. I want briefly to say what insights I have into it.

Paul says, "Flesh and blood cannot inherit the kingdom of God." One could say, "Dust to dust, earth to earth" [cf. Gen. 3:19; Eccl. 3:20; 12:7] and "Each *thing* has its time" [cf. Eccl. 3:1]. All that is perishable is an analogy of this truth. Considered in the light of Easter and measured by Jesus, all that we now are and all that we think and do, is insufficient and temporary. Remembering this clearly would save us a lot of disappointment and error, because then we would not *delude* ourselves in any way whatsoever about what is not and cannot be. This insight into the truth of human life may be *painful,* and yet we may recognize in it something that *spares* us pain. If the reality that Easter reveals were manifest in what presently exists, it would be unbearable; it would take the breath away. The few who have seen and heard something of the reality of God have been frightened to the point of death. But God does not want to strike us dead with this kingdom. Each thing *does have* its time, and it is God who gives us the analogy of perishable things. They reflect the great light in which we all live, and this is enough for us. But we must *know* that they are only a reflection and that we live entirely in what is temporary.

And now we come to what Paul calls *a mystery, a secret,* because it is a truth one never thinks about. "We will not all die, but we will all be changed." *Suddenly, in the twinkling of an eye,* at the sound of the last trumpet, the dead will be raised, and we will be changed. This is a remarkable moment. It encompasses both the dead and the living *at once,* so it is not a moment in time, neither in the year 2000 nor in the year 20,000, but a moment in eternity; and yet it was in time already before the year 2000 and before the year 20,000. *This moment is today,* but it was also yesterday and it will be tomorrow. It is *the moment, the day of Jesus Christ,* which is not a moment of time but ends all moments of time. In that eternal moment, on that day of Jesus Christ, *the answer,* the certainty, the new world, the life of the resurrection will break through for all people, just as it has broken through in Jesus Christ. On that day *the sun will rise,* while we today, seeing only the morning dawn, are only aware of its coming. *We will become* something other and new beyond flesh and blood, beyond what is perishable. Behind the human last *the divine first emerges. What in this moment becomes and is,* is being and truth; it is our being and our truth. *From God we are given the gift of being the heirs of his kingdom. Easter has to do with us.* "Thanks be to God, who gives us the victory!" Yes, victory, forgiveness, redemption, and eternal being before God and eternal walking in God's light [cf. Ps. 89:15].

Now we can understand our life. Paul says further, "*This perishable body must put on imperishability,* and this mortal body must put on immortality." The mystery, the secret, is to understand ourselves in God. Our whole life, both outside in the world and within us, *goes toward this moment. Everything that is transitory and passing aims* at what is perfect. The "beyond," the eternal, *hangs over* all that is here and now, all that is in time. Nothing is excepted, neither the great and significant nor the small and insignificant; neither the inner within us nor the outer of the world; neither personal duties and cares nor politics. As true as it is that all of this is perishable flesh and blood, so also it all strives, as in a great river, toward imperishability, the kingdom of God, and so toward what it should be by God's act in resurrection and being changed. There is no hair of our head that does not wish to join in [cf. Matt. 10:30 par.] Paul says, "This perishable body *must* put on imperishability!" It *must*! As it was said before: we *must* die, so now Paul says, we *must* live! All is meant as *life and living* in the world, a world that is now in perishing decomposition. As all *flowers* turn toward the sun, so all that is created, both the visible and the invisible, turns to its creator. Everything has its time, but it wants not only its time: it will also have *its eternity.* That is what we need to think about. We want to *follow* this tendency of all things toward imperishability. We want to be true to life, so that on that day of all days, the day of Jesus Christ, we may stand in honor and not shame with this perishable and mortal body that is now entrusted to us.

And when and where it occurs that by God's act Easter happens and Jesus is revealed as victor, there the promise is fulfilled that death is consumed in the victory, as is written, "Where, O death, is your victory? Where, O death, is your sting?" These are words of *great longing,* words of Advent from the Old Testament. Not only this great longing is fulfilled in the mystery of resurrection, but *all great longing* of human being. From the days of Abraham until today, what have human beings wished for and sought, believed and hoped for, but to go beyond what is humanly last and final. *Truly they seek not* what is questionable, insecure, and doubtful, although they seem to seek these; rather they truly want *death to be consumed* by victory, and that the divine first may overcome the human last. And *this is* and does happen in the moment, on the day of Jesus Christ, when the sun of Easter rises over us.

Why are we still in great longing? Because we are still *in death,* because flesh and blood cannot inherit the kingdom of God. "The sting of death is *sin.*" Whatever is flesh and blood, whatever is time, whatever is this side of eternity, is sin and falling away from the living God. Why are we still in sin? The power of sin is *the law.* Ever again sin makes us fear God, makes us serve God as servants and not in freedom, makes us put morality and religion in the place of the knowledge of perceptive insight, and makes us seek at best a human righteousness. In Jesus the law is ended [cf. Rom. 10:4], sin is forgiven, and dominion is taken from death [cf. 2 Tim. 1:10]. "Thanks be to God, who gives us the victory" in Jesus Christ.

The last part of the text is an admonition: "*Therefore, my beloved,* be steadfast, immovable, always excelling in the work of the Lord, because you know that in the Lord your labor is not in vain." Yes, if we can only take to heart this "*therefore*"! Who can be *steadfast,* in all the motion, agitation, instability, and upset of our life? Who can *excel* in the work of the Lord and know what the work is that needs to be done? Who can believe that our laborious work in this world, where all is perishable and only an analogy, is not *in vain*? Who can do it without knowing why it is not in vain? And why is it not? Therefore, dear brothers and sisters, therefore: *because Easter is,* because Jesus lives, because the last trumpet sounds, because the all-deciding Word of God has been spoken. *We can know the why,* and we can take the admonition to heart. Or should we really *not know* it? Then let us seek, ask, and knock at the door until we know it much, much better.

COMMENTS

"Listen, I will tell you a mystery!" It is as if that Pauline phrase drives Barth's 1920 Easter sermon. The preacher begins with an engaging series of rhetorical questions and sweeping assertions about the "enigma of Easter":

Do we want to risk coming close to the *enigma of Easter*? But can we not come close? For this enigma is also the entire *content of the Bible*. It has no other content than this: Easter, resurrection, out of death into life! If this were not the Bible's content, we could close it and lay it aside forever. If the Bible does not tell us this, it tells us nothing. And what it tells us is the whole *truth of Christianity*. Beside this truth, there is no room for any other. If Christianity did not carry this truth within it, it would have long since disappeared because of its weakness and lack of honesty. And that truth is also the *meaning of our whole existence*.

What Paul calls "mystery," Barth terms "enigma." The preacher confesses his incapacity to speak this enigma as strongly as it deserves for here is the whole significance of the Christian faith. Then he invites everyone, even those "here today who do not often attend church," to gaze with him at this enigmatic "high alpine mountain whose snowy peaks are veiled in clouds and mist." He demands that we look at "this mountain, even if we do not see it well."

In *Romans* Barth announced his intention to place himself "in a relation to his author of utter loyalty" (17). He will take Paul more seriously than any other commentary about Paul. There he praised Paul as no "genius rejoicing in his own creative ability" but rather as a herald who says what he is told to say, "an emissary, bound to perform his duty; the minister of his King; a servant, not a master" (27). Paul is one who has placed himself in complete submission to his King and thereby has had his world rocked; Barth intends to do the same. We hear echoes of *Romans* in this sermon. During these months Barth preached more or less sequentially through 1 Corinthians. He is definitely more stimulated by the Pauline correspondence than the Gospels or other narrative portions of Scripture. In my own experience, mainline liberal preachers gravitate toward the Gospels; evangelical, conservative preachers love Paul. In Barth's hands, Paul's resurrection testimony lives, becomes a challenge, an in-the-face assertion in the face of contemporary doubt.

Despite his introductory comments about enigma and mystery, in section 2 Barth moves toward strong, concise declarative assertions: "Easter is Jesus as he is, Jesus as victor: . . . not enlightenment, nor a model to imitate, nor a religion, nor a church that gives us the victory. It is Jesus. . . . That is Easter. . . . That is Jesus. He is victor. And that is Easter." Barth sounds more like an experienced preacher here, in full control of his rhetorical devices, more sure of where he wants to take us in the sermon.

Two engaging, counterintuitive claims are made in section 2: "Jesus stirs up the last doubt in us" and "Jesus places us in *a final insecurity*." Jesus causes doubt? Jesus makes us insecure? While one doesn't often hear such talk about Jesus from us contemporary preachers, these assertions are crucial to Barth's epistemology. Jesus is not the answer to all our questions, the solution to our problems; he is the one who provokes the questions and causes the problems that confront us with the living God. To stand before Jesus is to be cast into an epistemological crisis. To know Jesus is to know that in the deepest sense we do not know. Later in the sermon Barth says that the resurrected Christ is an event that produces "*restless disquiet*," a "final *shudder*." Worldly critics think they have raised some interesting questions about Jesus. Their modern, academic doubts are as child's play compared with the doubts that Jesus himself speaks "louder, more powerfully, and in a way that overturns everything." The questions that Jesus provokes are of more import than the merely utilitarian "Is this relevant to my life?" or the simply historical "How could this really happen?" Jesus' resurrection poses the fundamental question "What is true?" Our vaunted human search for goodness and truth gets "no further than the crucifixion of the Son of God," says the preacher, his voice dripping with sarcasm. Something about us face-to-face with Truth makes us want to kill it.

Speaking of Jesus as the "final insecurity" leads Barth to say that Jesus leads us "*to the final boundary*"—death. Death tells the truth about us. True wisdom is always some form of "death wisdom"—a favorite theme in the thought of Thurneysen and Barth. The resurrection is the event beyond all events because here we are confronted with the defeat of death, Paul's "last enemy" (1 Cor. 15:26). We cannot know the magnitude of that grand defeat if we don't truthfully acknowledge the Enemy.

Jesus brings us to this boundary, not for us to wallow in despair, but he shoves us to this boundary "in order [for it] to be *crossed*." Again he repeats, "Jesus is victor! That is Easter."

Then the preacher makes a move that I find rather baffling. In section 3 he digresses, "Let me make several remarks about our text." While his creative interpretation of Paul's "Flesh and blood cannot inherit the kingdom of God" is interesting, Barth undercuts much of its force by presenting his thoughts on the potential painfulness of Easter as a sort of aside. If the preacher had ended the sermon before this digression, I think it would have been a stronger sermon. The "mystery" and "enigma" would have been enjoyed as mystery and enigma rather than as occasion to treat the congregation to the preacher's thoughts on dialectical theology concepts like the "eternal moment."

I like Barth's existentializing of Paul's "We will all be changed" into his "eternal moment" whenever and wherever the resurrection breaks through to us and we are transformed by the vision of the truth of Easter. However, as it stands in this sermon, the thoughts are hard to follow, and the sermon definitely loses much of its energy in this section.

The last paragraph of the sermon discusses a typical Pauline move that we see in the text: a series of theological declarations is followed by Paul's "therefore." Then Paul launches into ethical implications of those theological assertions. I thought it would have been good for the preacher to say a bit more about the ethical implications of resurrection. If Jesus is Victor, if almighty death is defeated, how then shall we live?

True to himself, Barth appears reluctant to say much of anything about the ethical implications of all of this. He clearly believes that a sermon is to be theological and christological in focus, not anthropological. What God has done in Jesus Christ is so much more interesting and relevant than anything we are to do. True, Paul says only that we ought therefore to excel "in the work of the Lord" and "your labor is not in vain." And the preacher is content to leave it at that. But still it seems possible for the preacher to have said more. Throughout his career Barth was frequently criticized for putting forth a theology that undercut ethics. Some said that Barth so stressed the activity of God that he left little room or need for human response. I think he acquitted himself of that charge: while Barth's theologically based ethics was a challenge to much that passes for Christian ethics, still it was ethics. However, I was left wondering in what ways our work could be the Lord's work and why "because of Easter" our "labor is not in vain." I think Barth missed a grand opportunity, following Paul's "therefore," to demonstrate a theologically derived ethic. Then again, perhaps that is a criterion for good preaching; it leaves us with questions, suggests to us further sermons yet to be preached!

The sermon ends with one more enigmatic twist in which Barth characterizes the challenge of the Christian faith as a mostly noetic challenge: How do we know what we know about Christ? He answers that for some in the congregation, Easter means that we can know; for others Easter signifies that we really cannot know. If we know, we can now "take the admonition to heart." And if we don't know, then we must "seek, ask, and knock at the door until we know it much, much better."

What the congregation made of that, I don't know.

Barth's repeated use of a favorite phrase of his in this period—"Jesus is Victor!"—echoes the watchword of one of Barth's pastoral mentors, Johann Christoph Blumhardt (1805–80). The son of this prominent Lutheran preacher and faith healer was Christoph Blumhardt (1842–1919), whose death occurred the year before this sermon. The younger Blumhardt and Barth met for a series of formative conversations in 1915, just before Barth began his work on *Romans*. "Jesus is Victor!" figured prominently in a famous (among many of Barth's friends, an infamous) episode in which the elder Blumhardt, praying for a deeply troubled young woman, performed an exorcism in which the demonic spirit had left the woman while crying out, "Jesus is Victor!" This was an experience of the risen Christ on a scale that was unknown to Barth, very much against his orthodox, academic theology, casting the young Barth into scary but invigorating new theological territory.

That which impressed Barth about the younger Blumhardt, as he later explained, was that "Blumhardt always begins right away with God's presence, might, and purpose: he starts out from God; he does not begin by climbing upwards to Him by means of contemplation and deliberation."[1] From Blumhardt, Barth learned that theology commences with God, not with our pious human yearnings or experience. The God of Blumhardt's theology was a strong, active, invasive, disarmingly present God. "What is God doing in the world?" is more important than any of our questions about ourselves. Genuinely Christian thinking should focus not upon our supposed "religious experience," the infatuation of nineteenth-century theology, but upon God's actual signs and wonders in the world. Jesus is Victor, not only over sin and death, but also over all our contrived gods and vain means of climbing up to God.

Barth's politics was never the same after his encounters with Blumhardt. The thought—that we cannot ascend to God; only God can descend to us, and does so with world-shattering deeds of power—had the effect of moving Barth away from some of his rather tame youthful socialism and into a more radical assessment of the relationship of Christianity in the world. The most radically political statement we can make is when we are able to say, in the face of the world's politics, "Thy kingdom come!" The kingdom of God is a present reality that comes to us from beyond, a kingdom that precedes and judges all of our concepts and experiences of the kingdoms of this world, particularly religiously derived concepts of the kingdom of God.[2] The world with its present political arrangements does not simply need improvement; it needs radical, sweeping, eschatological transformation that only God can give. That transformation cannot be fully characterized with the available language and methods of socialist politics. Christianity demands its own distinctive speech to describe its distinctive vision. Part of the duty of a preacher is to foster the church's distinctive discourse, to teach people how to talk about God in ways that are congruent with the character of God as revealed in Jesus Christ. In these sermons, Barth is clearly teaching the church to think in a new way by teaching them how to use the church's peculiar speech. Easter means a whole new world.

Thus, standing behind this 1920 Easter sermon is the conviction that the resurrection is a world-shattering, deeply disruptive event that changes everything, disrupts everything, *now*. Paul is the man who woke up to a whole new world, and whenever we experience the resurrection, we do too. Easter is God here, God now. The resurrection is in history but is not of history, is not limited to history, and it cannot be apprehended through the methods of historical investigation. The resurrection is the supreme instance of the eternal breaking victoriously into the now. The God we meet in the risen Christ is not only loving but also powerful, active, an imperialistic One who is impossible to relegate to the safe realm of the personal, the private, or the spiritual. In the resurrection, Jesus is victorious, not only over death but also over the enemies of God. And sometimes God's most devious enemies are us. Our attempts to deceive ourselves about our deadly situation, our presumption that we can come to God on our own, that we can think about God by ourselves using our human capacities—all these certify our god-killing enmity. The good news is that Jesus is Victor not only over death, but also over sin, our sin. The resurrection proves to us not only that Jesus is raised but also that he shall reign. Here is truth that cannot be argued, much less proved. It must be asserted, proclaimed, which is what Barth did on an April day in 1920.

"Thanks be to God, who gives us the victory" in Jesus Christ.

Luke 2:33–35

And the child's father and mother were amazed at what was being said about him. Then Simeon blessed them and said to his mother Mary, "This child is destined for the falling and the rising of many in Israel, and to be a sign that will be opposed so that the inner thoughts of many will be revealed—and a sword will pierce your own soul too."

1. *The light shines:* That is the great *fact* of Christmas. Whoever has eyes that see, sees it shine. That is the great *possibility* of Christmas. So look then, and be a child of the light, now that you have the light! [cf. John 12:35–36]. That is the great *challenge* of Christmas: "Look and see!" All of this—the fact of the light, the possibility of seeing it, and the challenge—is placed before us in the *name Jesus* given to us as witness, power, and life. But "the light shines *in the darkness*" [John 1:5]. The night is not yet over; only a twilight indicates from whence the day will come, and only for those who look in the right direction. Between God and humanity still hangs the *curtain* of sin, world, and death. Yet a few in one place saw a bright light, a light that anyone behind the curtain would see, if they could and wanted to see. *The old* has not yet passed away, and look, there is nothing new [cf. 2 Cor. 5:17]—unless possibly there are persons who, although they are in the midst of the old, look toward the new and have it in sight, but only in sight.

2. How great is *the hiddenness of God,* who lets his light shine—shine in the darkness. How great is *the risk of believing* in this light that shines in the darkness. We may not think that, because of Christmas, God is less hidden or faith less of a risk, that Christmas has made God or faith *easier,* more comfortable and simple. The very opposite is true: *nowhere is God more hidden* than in Jesus Christ. For nowhere is it as clear as it is in Jesus that the real light of our life is *eternal* light, a light

to which our life is *not at all suited,* a light that completely *contradicts* our life, and light that we are *not able* to see. If we do see it, it is because a miracle is worked in us. In this light it is clear as nowhere else that we really are *in the night* and that the night is not over; that we are still separated from God by that curtain; that we exist *in an old being* that has not passed away; and that we can neither see, have, possess, nor enjoy what is new.

Furthermore *only in Jesus Christ* does *the nature of the risk of faith* become so completely clear. Where Jesus Christ is not known or where he has been forgotten, *there life is easy,* comfortable, and simple, and human beings think they know *all sorts of means,* bridges, and pathways to get from the world to God. But Jesus Christ says, "*I am the way,* and the truth, and the life. No one comes to the Father except through me" [John 14:6]. Where Christ is not known or has been forgotten, God is made *accessible,* inexpensive, cheap. With Christ, God is *inaccessible,* expensive, costly. Where Christ is not known or has been forgotten, one hears, "Come on, just trust in God and be good about it; it is possible for you, you'll see!" But here, where Christ is known, one hears, "*No, it is not possible,* it will not turn out right; and to trust in God means to *see light* where one sees only darkness; to *see life* where one sees only death; *to see yes* where one only sees no. To trust God means a *leap* into space where one sees only an abyss; it means to trust nothing but *God.* Can you do that? Will you do it? *Then come*!" Between God and those who say, "It is possible," stands the *crucified Christ,* and he says, "Yes, it is possible, but *through God* alone. And that is *the greatest of all risks:* to believe in God alone."

3. That is why old Simeon in the temple said of Jesus: "*This child is destined for the falling and rising of many in Israel!*" Like all serious friends of God, Simeon knew that when the relationship between God and human beings becomes *earnest,* when God lets God's light *shine* in the darkness, and when it is *seen,* then it becomes evident how great the mystery of God is, and how bold the courage must be that is required for belief in the God who thrones in mystery. When Simeon speaks of *Israel,* he means the people who already have a light and a relationship to God. Here today we would say it is Christianity that already has a light and a relationship to God.

But then according to Simeon in our text, there must be a *crisis* in Christianity, a crisis of life and death, as in a serious illness. And then

Christians must *choose*. *What do you want:* the *eternal*, true, and invisible light of God, or only the temporal, untrue, and visible lights that you have made? Do you want the light that must *shine ever anew* under unceasing sighing, calling, pleading, and waiting, or those lights that are always there and that one can have among so many other things one possesses? Do you want the light before which one can *only stand*, worship, and be silent? Or do you want the lights with which one may do anything one wants, lights that one can have close at hand with idle talk and doings, because they are our own lights? Do you want insight into what we will be, but which has not yet appeared [1 John 3:2], or the illusion that it is already day? Do you want the *means, bridges, and pathways* that only lead from one sickness to the next, from one darkness to the next, or do you want the abyss of reconciliation in Christ? Do you want what is cheap or what is costly? Do you want the faith that says, "*It is possible for you!*" or the faith that relies only on the belief that with God nothing is impossible? [cf. Luke 1:37]. Do you want, first and last, *the God* that human beings have made for themselves in their own thought, according to their own opinions and needs, or the true God, who thrones in mystery and who, when he becomes visible, works a miracle? *Jesus Christ compels* human beings to make this choice, especially those who have the most and are the most [in human estimation].

For the more they have and the more they are, the sharper must they turn to get around the corner, and they must turn the corner in order to see the eternal light and come to the knowledge of the true God. And the more they have and are, the sharper must the separation be between what is "from below" and what is "from above." Jesus Christ *is the either/or* that one cannot avoid. We have all heard a lot of sermons and read a lot of books, and yet we *notice nothing* of this either/or. We may take this as a sign that we have noticed very little of Jesus Christ. *If Jesus Christ speaks* with us, then we have before us the choice, the sharp corner, the separation, the either/or. At this point *those fall* who love the darkness more than the light, who in the darkness are quite content with their own lights. At the same point those persons arise who do not confuse light with darkness, but recognize light as light and darkness as darkness [cf. Isa. 5:20]. They would rather see their own lights extinguished than do without the eternal light that shines in the darkness.

4. And that is why, as Simeon says, this child is to be *a sign that will be opposed* and contradicted. Like all earnest friends of God, he knew

that there will be everywhere a loud, angry, and avid opposition, *when* God is again a mystery for human beings; when a person again needs a bold courage to believe in God; when God, so to speak, *withdraws* from human beings, becoming no longer familiar, superficial, and cheap, but wills *truly* to be God; when human beings recognize how much they must let go, indeed everything, in order to serve God in Spirit and in truth [cf. John 4:24]. When this *crisis* comes to human beings, then Jesus is and will be angrily opposed, just as Saul opposed him in his heart before he became Paul [Acts 9:1–22; 22:3–16; 26:9–18]. Wherever a person risks taking on this crisis, this either/or, and representing it to others purely and clearly, there all humanity's *passion*, indignation, and anger will break out of their hidden recesses; and they will do so most violently among those who have the most and are the most, because they have the most to lose.

What a shock it is when we truly realize that the lights we have cherished are not eternal light, and that they are better done without. The means, bridges, and pathways we have used for ourselves *lead nowhere;* we are better off turning around and going where only the abyss opens before us. Our faith is *not faith,* and our God is *not God.* We must *repent,* particularly we who are something and have something and cannot see the light in the darkness. With all our supposed wealth, we are poor, *poor in God* [cf. Luke 12:21]. If we are told this, must we not cry out *with all our heartfelt might* against the speaker? "You take everything from us and give us nothing; you let us hunger in the desert [cf. Exod. 16:3]; you touch what is most holy in us; you are a destroyer [cf. Mark 1:24 par.], a spoiler of temples [cf. Mark 14:58 par.], and a blasphemer! [Mark 14:64 par.]. *Jesus Christ was the speaker* who called to repentance; he was the crisis, the either/or. And that is why all those accusations and curses that we have just heard were shouted at him. That is why he was a sign that was opposed and contradicted.

Let us not think too quickly that we would not have shouted at him and not contradicted him. For we must *all the more* oppose and contradict the eternal light the more we have our own lights, the more beautiful the names we give them are, the better they help us forget that we are in darkness, the more we depend on them in our heart, and the less willing we are to let them be taken from us. Indeed, it would be better for us if we could become aware that we must contradict Jesus Christ. Perhaps the way to resurrection leads through the opposition and contradiction, as Paul's life demonstrates. There are such *sad books* and such *poor preachers* who talk as if their readers and listeners will simply nod in agreement. They have not recognized that Jesus Christ is *the sign that is opposed and contradicted.* And if they have not recognized this, so also they have recognized nothing of the either/or, of the path that goes sharply around the corner. And so also they have not recognized that it is the eternal light that in Jesus enters into the world and gives it a new brightness!

5. This is the sword that, according to Simeon, *will pierce the soul of Mary.* Readers of these words have rather always understood them as a reference to the *suffering of Christ* and the sorrow that it causes his mother. But we want to understand this reference in its complete significance. Mary certainly wished *another way* for her son. She would rather *not have seen him as the sign* that would be opposed and contradicted. She hoped to see him deliver *his message* smoothly, directly, peacefully, and in a friendly manner, and conclude his life with full and *satisfying success.* She was not prepared to see the one at whose birth the angels sang be rejected by the whole world and be tortured to death on the cross of shame. If that was to be the sign that was contradicted, who of us would not rather agree with Mary's question about *why Christ had to suffer these things?* [cf. Luke 24:26].

Yet if he did not have to suffer them, he would *not have been the eternal light,* not *the Son* of the hidden God, and not *the initiator* of bold and daring faith [cf. Heb. 12:2]. The sword that pierced the soul of Mary and that pierces all our hearts, when we clearly understand how gladly we too would have had Christ without the cross—this sword is the *sword of the Word of God* [cf. Heb. 4:2]. It must bring what is mortal from life to death. *The wish for other lights must die,* as must the wish for other paths, for another faith, another God. God speaks where we are silent. God begins where we end. God lives where we die. *Did Christ not have* to suffer these things in order to enter his glory? [Luke 24:26]. As the sign that is opposed and contradicted, he is the *sign of our reconciliation* with God. As the crucified one who draws us into his death, he is the *light that shines in the darkness.*

6. "*So that the inner thoughts of many will be revealed!*" What *thoughts* of our hearts are revealed if we *perceive* who Christ is, and what sort of fire has he come to kindle on earth? [cf. Luke 12:49]. Perhaps *thoughts of opposition and contradiction;* perhaps a welling up of our pride, of our self-awareness, and our deepest sensitivity? I say again, *if our inner thoughts were revealed!* If, in deepest awareness of what we are opposing and

contradicting, it burned within us to say "No" to Jesus Christ! From this burning "No" there would be but a short step to "Yes," shorter than from the emptiness of our present yes. But perhaps not thoughts of opposition and contradiction, but *thoughts of joy,* of thankfulness, and of fulfilled expectation. Is it not finally *just what we seek:* the eternal light? Have we perhaps become tired of our own lights? *Do we perhaps not know* that with all these lights we are miserable, poor, and naked in the darkness?

After all the disappointments and shame that we have behind us, is there not in us human beings of the present time a *deep longing* for the true, the unknown, and incomprehensible God? Is there not in us a deep longing for the God to whom one can entrust oneself, because this God is God? *Do we not have enough* of all the false calm, appeasement, and consolation, with which we imagine ourselves being something and possessing something? Are we not *ripe for directing our eyes toward that being and having* that await us in eternity in the resurrection and in the kingdom of God, the kingdom that wills to come from heaven to earth? If we perceive who Christ is, could not precisely *these thoughts of our hearts* be revealed? Dear friends, *both must be revealed:* the opposition and contradiction, and the joy. If only *our* thoughts may be revealed exactly where *God's* thoughts in Christ were revealed! For what Paul has written is true: "Everything that is revealed is light!" [Eph. 5:13].

COMMENTS

The babe whom old Simeon presents to us on Christmas 1920 is also the Crucified. Taking his cue from Simeon's prediction, "This child is destined for the falling and the rising of many," Barth in this sermon links Christmas and Good Friday, juxtaposes incarnation with atonement. Thus we meet an unexpected, even undesired Savior.

I believe that we can understand Barth's homiletic intentions here only through reference to Feuerbach. Barth believed that Ludwig Feuerbach (1804–72) was fundamentally correct when he claimed that the Christian religion, or any religion for that matter, was the result of a delusional attempt to project our wishes upon something called "God." We inflate our desires, the ways we wish the world could be, and then bow down to this concoction called "religion." "Spirit" is simply the human spirit projected into infinity. Theology is only inflated and self-deceiving anthropology.

Feuerbach was a fierce critic of Christianity, yet his critique provided Barth with the insight he needed to assail the liberal theology of his student years. In an article he wrote in 1926 (published in 1927), Barth praised Feuerbach for astutely unmasking the problem of theology. What Barth liked most in Feuerbach was not his notorious idea that Christianity was a mere projection of human religious yearnings, but rather Feuerbach's bald reduction of theology to nothing but anthropology, thus typifying the fate of most theology of the age. Theology had degenerated into anthropology, beginning with various assessments of the "human condition" rather than with "And God said . . ." Feuerbach furthered a process that began in Kant. As Barth saw it, Feuerbach merely exposed theology's nasty little secret: it had become more interested in humanity than in God. From Feuerbach, Barth learned his famous dictum that theology must be more than talking about humanity in a very loud voice. Otherwise, Feuerbach's charge against "theology" would simply be confirmed by our "theologians" themselves.

Agreeing with Feuerbach, D. F. Strauss (1808–74) wrote that religion is otherworldly fantasy based mostly on subjective projection of human needs. What passes for history in the New Testament is completely untrustworthy "poeticizing." Religion is interesting as a commentary upon human dreams but has no relationship to reality. Strauss had said (in his 1864 *The Life of Jesus Presented for the German People*) that the Sermon on the Mount had some continuing value because it expressed the "inner truth" of human conscience. "Christ-religion must be transformed into the religion of humanity," he declared. The resurrection of Christ is little more than "world-historical humbug." German scholarship can retrieve from Jesus a few universal, humanistic truths; otherwise Jesus himself is mostly pious fiction. Strauss compared the "religious domain" of the modern nineteenth-century German mind with the shrinking lands of the Native Americans in the United States. Modern thought is depriving religion of places to hide; human subjectivity is the last refuge of those intellectual holdouts who still cling to some sense of the spiritual.[1]

Barth's withering, relentless attack upon "religion" stems not only from his conviction of the axiomatic nature of the First Commandment against the fabrication of "other gods" but also because he thought that Feuerbach was right: "religion" is a sinful sham. Rather than bringing us close to God, religion is our most insidious defense against the true and living God.

I agree with Barth that much that passes for theology today validates Feuerbach's charge. Schleiermacher's relegation of theology to our subjectivity (he said that theology in the modern world must be an exploration of our "consciousness of God") is a hard habit to shake. In our day, finding the God of orthodox Christianity difficult to swallow, so-called "progressive Christianity" fashions a different god, one more congenial to thinking people whose thinking is constrained by the canons of modernity.[2] Others, believing that we Americans are an exceptional race, a people of good intentions and wholesome values, concoct a god who waves the flag and blesses patriotic self-righteousness as a Christian virtue. "NEED PEACE, COMFORT, AND ANSWERS?" asks a highway billboard near my home. Then it lists the church Web site. Jesus is whatever it is that you think you really, really need.

If you want to know the major reason why Barth so stressed the objectivity of the biblical text in his preaching, why he was so determined not to take his eyes off the text, why he resisted any temptation to make the text more accessible and congenial to his listeners—surely it was because he wanted to show that though Feuerbach was right about most "religion," he was wrong about Christ. Christian theology and preaching must be rescued from the radical subjectivity that only validates Feuerbach's charge. Jesus Christ is more than some collective projection of human wishes. He is a "fact." Jesus is the Lord who comes to us, not from out of us, coming as the Stranger who is unknown, unsought, unwelcomed.

In this Christmas sermon, Simeon presents us with the Savior we did not want. If we were projecting a God with whom to console ourselves, we certainly would not have projected the one in Luke 2:33–35!

The sermon begins affirmatively with the "*fact* of Christmas" as "the light shines *in the darkness.*" This "fact" (note the preacher's characterization of the Nativity as a "fact") is "the great *challenge* of Christmas." But then rather abruptly the preacher switches from the metaphor of "light" to that of "hiddenness." He exclaims, "How great is *the hiddenness of God.*" I dare say when most of us preachers think of Christmas, we think of it as the most accessible season of the Christian year. The crowds are certainly larger at Christmas Eve services. Christmas appears to have replaced Easter as the summit of the church year, judging from the size of the congregations. "Peace" has become the predominate Christmas-card sentiment. The season is said to bring out the best in everybody. Christmas is the only Christian festival wherein we receive any boost, even a passing nod, from the media or pop culture. Even if you can't figure out Jesus, Yuletide TV specials imply, you can still keep Christmas.

Barth obviously will have no such sentimental rubbish. Christmas is not a vague feeling; it is a stark "fact," but a most paradoxical, contradictory sort of fact. Barth pours forth a stream of polarities, paradoxes, contradictions, and enigmas in an attempt to do justice to the incarnation. To say that God has become a human being is like seeing light in darkness. We get a typically Barthian contention that God's utter inaccessibility and incomprehensibility is nowhere more apparent than in God's full revelation in Christ. A crucified Messiah? "*Nowhere is God more hidden* than in Jesus Christ."

Whereas it is popular today for purpose-driven, prosperity preachers to commend Jesus as the solution to our problems, the key to a happier life, and a technique for getting whatever it is we happen to crave, more than Jesus (Feuerbach *ascendit!*), Barth says that the only way to think such drivel is never to have actually met Jesus. The preacher has contempt for these who, by forgetting Jesus, contrive to make God "*accessible, inexpensive, cheap.*" Ouch.

There is a reason why Joel Osteen rarely refers to Jesus in his sermons. As old Simeon said, the "fact" of Jesus occasioned the "falling and the rising of many in Israel." Barth uses this as an opportunity to mine a theme that he worked so well in *Romans:* when someone in the New Testament like Simeon says "Israel," what he means is "church." Israel is any people who presume to have seen the "light" and to have a "relationship with God." The coming of Christ is judgment upon "Israel" and an end to all "religion," the exposure and unmasking of all humanly constructed attempts to climb up to God. The incarnation— encounter with God in the flesh—forces us to choose. Will we have God on our terms, "The God that human beings have made for themselves in their own thought, according to their own opinions and needs, or the true God, who . . . when he becomes visible, works a miracle?" The lowly God who is born at Bethlehem, the babe who seems to us as no god at all, compels this crisis. Either we shall be met by God as God is and be blinded by this peculiar light, or we shall continue to stumble in the dark with gods of our own devising.

"*What a shock* it is when we truly realize that the lights we have cherished are not eternal light. . . . The means, bridges, and pathways . . . *lead nowhere.*"

Later Barth said that the First Commandment (no other gods before God, the prohibition against idols) is "the first axiom of theology."

That axiom holds true for Barth even on Christmas. Every sermon, at any season in the church year, bows to the demands of the First Commandment and makes war on our idolatry. Surely there were some in the Christmas congregation at Safenwil who cried out against the preacher, as they cried in Exodus, "You take away everything from us and give us nothing," you "spoiler of temples." Awash, as we are at Christmas, in a sea of saccharine sentimentality, few seasons of the year are more suitable for sermons on idolatry.

Even mother Mary is not immune from Barth's critique. She hopes for another way for her son, a way that will not be as a sword through her heart. Mary was unprepared for the baby who was welcomed by angels eventually to be the man "tortured to death on the cross of shame." Christmas is thus a confrontation with death as much as a celebration of birth: "*The wish for other lights must die,* as must the wish for other paths, for another faith, another God."

We could in no way climb up to God, so God climbed down to us, appearing miraculously before us as the God we don't want. In this dying to our idolatries is our true light and life. With hardly a wave of the hand, Barth dismisses most modern theologies of this and that. Our contemporary theologies whisper to us that, while God may be God, dwelling in light inaccessible, at least we can climb up to God by way of our gender, our correct doctrine, our biblical principles, our stunning insights about the human condition, our politics of the right or the left, the blessed Eucharist, spiritual disciplines, Christian practices, our countercultural community, or even our collective experience of poverty and oppression. All this, claiming to be light, is testimonial to our idolatrous darkness.

Which renders a bit strange Barth's concluding comments. Is it true that we have a "*deep longing* for the true . . . God"? Is our age "*ripe*" for the "kingdom that wills to come from heaven to earth"? Such talk, after so devastating a Yuletide critique, suggests that Barth isn't quite done with the possibility of a valid human aspiration for the divine. Perhaps there is no way for a preacher, even the most anti-idolatrous Barthian, to be free of yearning for a point of contact, a bridge, a lifeline thrown out from here to the living, free God, particularly at Christmas.

Or perhaps those who have, in our darkness, caught a glimpse of the light find our best selves illumined, even if dimly, fleetingly in such light, particularly at Christmas, so that it is fair to speak of us as those who indeed "long for the true God."

"Everything that is revealed is light!"

In reading this Christmas sermon, as with many of these early sermons, I find myself torn between thinking that Barth presents his congregation with an obtuse, baffling, utterly elusive God beyond all comprehension and thinking that Barth's interpretation of Scripture presents a God who is effusive, effulgent, constantly disclosing, and eager to be seen through every passage of the Bible, anywhere we look. Revelation is linked to hiddenness. The light shines in the darkness, and the darkness, though it has not quenched the light, still contends against the light. We preachers must acknowledge the hiddenness and at the same time admit the light.

In his preface to the second edition of *Romans*, Barth said that the Bible's subject matter was the "infinite qualitative distinction" between time and eternity, between God and the human (10). God is not easily comprehended by humanity, certainly never comprehended by some act of human comprehension. God is hidden and remains hidden, even in God's self-disclosure, especially there.

And yet Barth is a preacher whose business it is to testify to the "fact" of God in Jesus Christ. The darkness, for all its power, cannot overcome the light. We must acknowledge revelation as revelation. Later, in *Church Dogmatics*, Barth warned against that sort of prideful agnosticism that is nothing less than "blasphemy against the Holy Spirit," in which we arrogantly "try to value our incapacity more highly than the capacity which God Himself in His revelation confers upon our incapacity."[3] Barth was at pains to clarify that when we speak of "God's hiddenness," we are not speaking of a general human incapacity of knowledge about God; we are testifying to the nature of God.[4] It is the hiddenness that is inherent whenever the Trinity is experienced as the Second Person of the Trinity—fully God and fully human. Hiddenness is not "behind revelation, but in it."[5] An old man, giving thanks for a baby through talk of swords, falling and rising, and opposition is the sort of enigmatic testimony required by the advent of a crucified God.

Which perhaps makes it all the more joyful when, by the end of this sermon, Barth lays aside his intellectual reservations, his epistemological struggles, his repressed aggravation with his uncomprehending congregation and with compromised and accommodated contemporary theology and simply, exuberantly proclaims the gospel. As Barth said later, we are not to attempt to prove revelation or to argue it, but rather we are to give thanks and grateful acknowledgment, full of joy and wonderment, that God loves us enough to speak.[6] Revelation does come because God is not only hidden, but also love. We must be honest about the "opposition and the contradiction" as well as "the joy," yes, the joy.

Everything that is ever revealed anywhere to anybody in a sermon "is light."

Notes

Introduction

1. All the biographical detail that follows comes from chap. 3, "Comrade Pastor," of Eberhard Busch's biography of Barth, *Karl Barth: His Life from Letters and Autobiographical Texts*, trans. John Bowden (Grand Rapids: Wm. B. Eerdmans Publishing Co., 1975).

2. For a look at Barth as preacher before 1917, see Arthur C. Cochrane, "The Sermons of 1913 and 1914," in *Karl Barth in Re-View: Posthumous Works Reviewed and Assessed*, ed. H. Martin Rumscheidt (Pittsburgh: Pickwick Press, 1981), 1–5.

3. Karl Barth, *The Theology of Schleiermacher*, trans. G. W. Bromiley (Edinburgh, T&T Clark, 1982), 264.

4. Quoted in Andreas Pangritz, *Karl Barth in the Theology of Dietrich Bonhoeffer*, trans. Barbara and Martin Rumscheidt (Grand Rapids: Wm. B. Eerdmans Publishing Co., 2000), 36.

5. Several of Barth's addresses in *The Word of God and Word of Man* (Boston: Pilgrim Press), first published in English in 1928, are from the same time period as the sermons in this collection.

6. At various points in my commentary on Barth's sermons, I will cite the English translation of the 2nd edition of *Romans*, by Edwyn C. Hoskyns, *The Epistle to the Romans* (London: Oxford University Press, 1933). All my citations, with numbers in parentheses, are from the English edition. For purposes here, the differences between the 1st and 2nd editions are not as important as the continuity. Barth worked on the 1st edition while he preached the 1917–18 sermons and defended and expanded *Romans* throughout this period until the 2nd edition, 1922. On the relationship between the 1st and 2nd editions, see Bruce L. McCormack, *Karl Barth's Critically Realistic Dialectical Theology: Its Genesis and Development 1909–1936* (Oxford: Oxford University Press, 1995).

7. In 1919 Barth and Thurneysen published a volume of sermons, *Suchet Gott, so werdet Ihr leben!* (2nd ed. 1928). One of these sermons is translated in the present volume: the Easter sermon of April 8, 1917. They also published another volume of sermons, preached between 1920 and 1924, which has been translated: *Come Holy Spirit*, trans. G. W. Richards (New York: Round Table, 1933).

8. I made extensive use of John E. Wilson's fine book in some of my comments on the background for Barth's sermons. John E. Wilson, *Introduction to*

Modern Theology: Trajectories in the German Tradition (Louisville: Westminster John Knox Press), 2007.

9. William H. Willimon, *Conversations with Barth on Preaching* (Nashville: Abingdon Press, 2006).

March 4, 1917

1. Busch, *Karl Barth*, 116.
2. Karl Barth, *The Word of God and the Word of Man*, trans. Douglas Horton (New York: Harper & Brothers, 1957), 28–50.

April 8, 1917

1. Goethe, *Faust* 1.5.737–741.
2. I should not overdo Barth's departure from his Kantian, Schleiermachian roots. In Barth's preoccupation with issues of epistemology and subjective appropriation of the Christian faith in these early sermons, he still stands within the nineteenth–century romantic, German liberal tradition of Schleiermacher. Although Barth reworked some of the nineteenth–century themes in some remarkable ways, even in that reworking he is a modern theologian. See Bruce L. McCormack, *Orthodox and Modern: Studies in the Theology of Karl Barth* (Grand Rapids: Baker Academic, 2008).

April 29, 1917

1. McCormack says, "In the years prior to the outbreak of the First World War," Barth's solution to the problem of the knowledge and availability of God "followed that of Herrmann in precise detail." See ibid., 27.
2. Quoted by McCormack in ibid., 22, with original emphasis.

March 3, 1918

1. The NRSV reads "acceptable" and "spiritual worship" instead of "well pleasing" and "reasonable worship." Barth is here using the common German translation of the Greek, both the Luther and the Zurich Bible (Froschauer) versions.
2. Editor's note: Barth is probably thinking especially of the dissolution of private ownership of land without compensation, decreed by the Soviet Congress in November 1917.
3. Karl Barth, *Homiletics*, trans. Geoffrey W. Bromiley and Donald E. Daniels (Louisville: Westminster John Knox, 1991), 69–70.

December 22, 1918

1. The NRSV has "overcome" instead of "comprehend." Because "comprehend" (as in the German and KJV) is important in the sermon, it is used here.

2. The winter of 1918 saw the worst influenza epidemic in modern history and brought many deaths. The war had brought greater economic hardship to industrial towns like Safenwil than they had experienced before. The citizen army had been mobilized, to defend Swiss neutrality if necessary, which meant a reduction in industrial production and workers' pay. Inflation rose sharply, and needed imported goods were in short supply. The general strike in November 1918 was put down by the army.

February 9, 1919

1. See Eberhard Busch, *Karl Barth and the Pietists: The Young Karl Barth's Critique of Pietism and Its Response,* trans. D. W. Bloesch (Downers Grove, IL: InterVarsity Press, 2004).

2. Dietrich Bonhoeffer, *Worldly Preaching,* ed. Clyde E. Fant (Nashville: Thomas Nelson, 1975), 125.

January 18, 1920

1. Karl Barth, *The Epistle to the Romans,* trans. Edwyn C. Hoskyns, 6th ed. (London: Oxford University Press, 1933), 332.

February 29, 1920

1. The way preaching arises out of and drives us back to Christology is worked out well by Michael P. Knowles, *We Preach Not Ourselves: Paul on Proclamation* (Grand Rapids: Brazos Press, 2008). Knowles interprets 2 Corinthians in a wonderfully Barthian manner.

April 4, 1920

1. See Dorrien's discussion of Barth and Blumhardt in Gary Dorrien, *The Barthian Revolt in Modern Theology: Theology without Weapons* (Louisville, KY: Westminster John Knox Press, 2000), 40–41. See also Busch, *Karl Barth and the Pietists,* 31–33.

2. Dorrien, *Theology without Weapons,* 53–54.

December 26, 1920

1. See the section on Strauss in John E. Wilson, *Introduction to Modern Theology: Trajectories in the German Tradition* (Louisville: Westminster John Knox, 2007), 70–74.

2. For a self-definition of "Progressive Christianity," see http://www.tcpc.org. The Web site lists the "Eight Points of Progressive Christianity." There is also a magazine, *Progressive Christian,* info@tpcmagazine.org. I think it fair

to say that "progressive" in this context is to be taken to mean the last gasp of nineteenth–century social–gospel liberalism—Feurbach triumphant.

3. Karl Barth, *Church Dogmatics* [*CD*], trans. G. W. Bromiley et al., 5 vols. in 14 (Edinburgh: T&T Clark, 1936–62, 1977), II/I:201.

4. *CD* II/1:183.

5. Karl Barth, *The Göttingen Dogmatics*, trans. G. W. Bromiley (Grand Rapids: Wm. B. Eerdmans Publishing Co., 1991–), 1:93.

6. *CD* II/1:216–20.

Index of Names

Abraham, 82, 139
Adam and Eve, 69
Amos, 18, 67
Augustine, 57

Baptist, John the, 37, 82, 84, 99–101, 106–7
Bartimaeus, 1
Bloesch, D. W., 159n1
Blumhardt, C., xii, 159n1
Blumhardt, J. C., xii
Bonhoeffer, D., xii, 75, 109, 157n4, 159n2
Bowden, J., 157n1
Brodie, B., xvii
Brodie, K., xvii
Bromiley, G. W., 157n3, 158n3, 160n3, 160n5
Bultmann, R., 32, 34
Busch, E., 157 n1, 158n1, 159n1

Calvin, 100
Cochrane, A. C., 157 n2

Daniels, D. E., 158n3
Darwin, 23
Dorrien, G. P., 159n1, 159n2
Dostoyevsky, xiii, 12

Elijah, 100, 123

Fant, C. E., 159n2
Feuerbach, L., 150–53, 160n2
Fosdick, H. E., 35
Freud, S., 23

Goethe, 158n1

Hauerwas, S. M., 24, 129
Herrmann, W., 32–35, 158n1
Horton, D., 158n2
Hosea, 119
Hoskyns, E. C., 157n6, 159n1
Hüssy, W., ix

Isaiah, 82, 100

Jeremiah, 82, 100
Joel, 67, 119
Judas, 20
Jung, C. G., 23

Kaiser W., xi
Kant, I., 23, 151, 158n2
Kierkegaard, S., xiii, 9, 45, 119
Knowles, M. P., 159n1
Kutter, H., xvi

Lindbeck, G., 34
Luther, M., 8, 33, 49, 100

Mark, 9
Marx, K., 23
Mary, 149
Matthew, 100, 103
McCormack, B. L., 157n6, 158n2, 158n1, 158n2
McKim, D., xiii
Milbank, J., 121
Moses, 82, 100

Nietzsche, F., xi

Oetinger, F., 135
Osteen, J., 35, 44, 153

161

Index of Subjects